Our Weekend Jacket

Intended for weekend wear in spring and summer, this good looking Jacket lets the compulsive or obsessive executive know when he is not at the office. Raglan sleeve construction combines trim, easy fit with insufficient pocket space for wallet, papers, pens, and credit cards. Waist length of about 25″ is too short for anything but a leisure garment. Vest wearage and linen display at cuff look very foolish with this Jacket, increasing evidence to wearer that he is to relax. Knit-lined stand-up collar can be buttoned snugly if lack of necktie causes anxiety. Two-button flapped handwarmer pockets will not hold anything more substantial than a candy bar or two tickets to game. Dry Clean or let get dirty. Two colors: Natural Tan. Easy-goin' Navy. Men's sizes: S. M. L. XL. Smaller sizes will fit most Women executives.

TGIF   Our Weekend Jacket, $51.45 ppd.

More Items from Our Catalog®

By Alfred Gingold
Photographs by Dan Nelken

Our Staff
Cover Illustration: Tom Beecham
Art Director: Deborah Bracken
Cover & Book Design: David M. Nehila
Design Assistant & Photo Stylist: René-Julien Aussoleil

Our Thanks
The Proprietor of Our Store would like to express Large Model Thanks to Rene Aussoleil, Deborah Bracken, Elmore James, Petra Morrison, David Nehila, Dan Nelken, Helen Rogan and Gabrielle Tessler.

Model thanks to Big Al, Rene Aussoleil, Ben Baglio, Barbara Becker, Eve Becker, Lisa Berkower, Rusty Berkower, Tom Rosica, Deb Bracken, Waldo Bracken, Adele Brown, John, Pamela & Oliver Buskin, Greg Correll, Yolande Flesch, Marilyn Friedman, Matthew Greene, Marcia Leonard, Bruce Michel, Max & Alix Michel, Emily Moss, Dave Nehila, Dan Nelken, Ana Rodriguez, Helen Rogan, Ted Stevenson Gabrielle Tessler, Susan Wasserstein, Jeff & Dan Weiss, and Hilary White.

MORE ITEMS FROM OUR CATALOG is an original publication of Avon Books. This work has never before appeared in book form.

AVON BOOKS
A division of
The Hearst Corporation
1790 Broadway
New York, New York 10019

Produced by Cloverdale Press,
133 Fifth Avenue, New York, N.Y. 10003

Copyright © 1983 by Big Al Enterprises, Inc.
and Cloverdale Press, Inc.
Published by arrangement with Big Al Enterprises, Inc. and Cloverdale Press, Inc.
Library of Congress Catalog Number: 83-91096
ISBN: 0-380-84657-8

Make-Up on page 68 by Dana Mills
Props on pages 8-9, 17, 25, 38, 45, 58,
    66-67, 70 by Marilyn Jean Friedman
Esoteric Research: Petra Morrison

Photo Credit on page 83 by Edward Stevenson
Photo Credits on page 29-30 by Leo De Wys, Inc.
Drawings on page 47 by Pui Ying Cheung

First Avon Printing, October, 1983

AVON TRADEMARK REG. U. S. PAT. OFF. AND IN OTHER COUNTRIES, MARCA REGISTRADA, HECHO EN U. S. A.

Printed in the U. S. A.

DON 10 9 8 7 6 5 4 3 2 1

Browser Fly

Skillful plastic replica of Our Catalog looks and moves like real paper. Will not sog or fade under water. Brightly colored illustrations and hilarious text provide ample distraction from hook. Trolled slowly through water, Fly draws many types of fish with promise of easy gift solution or self-giggleage. Weight, 1 smidge.

TEEHEE   Browser Fly $5.95 ppd.

Season's Greetage

On behalf of Our Store as well as Our many friends, relatives, and creditors, allow Us to thank you for the extraordinary reception Our Catalog has received across this great, not to mention extremely large, country of Ours. After years of struggle, industry, and sacrifice, success has come to Our neck of the woods, and it's a good feeling. Some of us have bought new tires. Others have taken up a second language. In consequence of a foot tracing sent to Us by a young dancer from San Francisco, the entire mail room now studies ballet. Even Our Store itself has changed. What was once a dank little shed, catering largely to muddled tourists searching for clean rest rooms and intact whaling villages, has grown into a spacious, department-type Store boasting the largest number of indoor electrical outlets in New England.

Still, some things remain the same. Since 1911 We have always believed in Old World traditions of painstaking craftsmanship, relentless attention to detail, and time and a half for overtime. Of course, Our Staff's union, Craftsfolk Local #207, insists on a work day riddled with half a dozen coffee breaks, a 90-minute lunch hour, and a brief recess followed by nap time! The union says the schedule insures Our Staff's undivided attention on the job; We call it Theory Zzzzz, but it is the only way We can be certain that Our items will live up to Our Guarantee. The unfortunate result of Our refusal to compromise Our standards, or even listen to reason, is a 3 year backlog of orders waiting to be filled.

There is no order form in this edition of Our Catalog; We're simply too busy to deal with any more just now. Please don't try to call Us, either; We've had Our number changed and it's unlisted. Cash, jewelry and gold teeth are still cheerfully accepted, however, and donated promptly to Our Research and Development Fund. Please feel free to give and give generously, knowing that you are aiding Us in Our ceaseless (since 1911) quest, to provide you with more and more and still more items of high quality, ingenious design, and obscure purpose. All contributions guaranteed tax-debatable.

Orthodox Bush Hat

Made for Us by the El-Al Bohne Company of Williamsburg, New York, hatters since you shouldn't ask, this good-looking Hat allows concentration, study, and prayer in tropical climates. Fine-woven nylon netting keeps out mosquitos and no-see-ums, provides clear view of text and commentary. Heavy-weight Sovereign quality fur felt with 2½" brim gives good protection during monsoons, hurricanes, or if, just in case, there's a sudden cold snap, you should at least have a warm Hat. Traditional styling is acceptable to Satmar, Babov, or Lubavitch sects.

One color: Strictly Black. Wt. 20 oz.
Four sizes: Pisher; Mensch; Chachem; Rebbe.

GLATT Orthodox Bush Hat,
for you only $57.44 ppd.

Hemispherical Fellowship T-Shirts

These colorful T-Shirts celebrate the unity, warm relations, and fundamental equality that exists among American nations. Each Shirt has a one-color, amusing declaration, which may or may not reflect wearer's sentiments or country of origin, silkscreened onto the front. Shirts are made on traditional patterns from cotton that is grown on Alabaman plantations, woven into fabric in Mexican sweatshops, and hand-squeegeed by Ottawan craftspersons. Will not shrink or fade for life of hemisphere.

Four models: White with "Kiss me, I'm American!" in blue letters. Red with "Kiss me, I'm Canadian!" in white letters. Blue with "Embrasse-moi, je viens du Québec!" in white letters. Camouflage with "¡Bésame, yo vengo de América Latina!" in white letters. Wt. about 7 oz.

US   White Hemispherical Fellowship T-Shirt, **$6.50 ppd.**
MAPLS   Red Hemispherical Fellowship T-Shirt, **$6.50 ppd.**
KNUKS   Blue Hemispherical Fellowship T-Shirt, **$6.50 ppd.**
THEM   Camouflage Hemispherical Fellowship T-Shirt, **$6.50 ppd.**

Up Down Vest

Depressive personalities in cool climates will appreciate this sporty Vest, which is filled with 5 ounces of high quality goose down and 3 ounces of freeze-dried laughing gas. Light in weight and easily packed, Vest provides enough warmth and jolliness to cover a wide range of weather conditions and emotional climates. May be worn unbuttoned or simply held over mouth and nose in warm weather. Wind-resistant nylon taffeta allows gradual gas release for up to three months. Nitrous oxide refurbishment Available. Snap front closure provides amusing distraction while waiting for morale to lift or just noodling.
Four colors: Bright Red. Bright Powder Blue. Bright Navy Blue. Bright Dark Green.
Four sizes: Sm. Med. Lg. Ex-lg. Sm.-er sizes will fit most Wmn.

TA-DAH!   Up Down Vest, $98.99 ppd.

Lice Infested Crew Necks

These attractive, lightweight 100% cotton Sweaters are infested with thousands of insect larvae which are invisible to the naked eye. As eggs hatch and grow, wearer becomes puzzled and often disturbed by mysterious, incessant itching. Eventually, wearer must delouse self and clean Sweater. Dry Clean only. Tasteful leisure wear for masochists, zealots, or the very hairy, who may find Sweater tickles. Also makes excellent gift for employers, in-laws, or former loved ones. Wt. 14 oz. (Weight of mature vermin not included).
Four colors: Natural Disaster. Sadie Maize. Disciplined Navy. Pee Green.
Four sizes: S.M.L.XL. S. and M. sizes should fit most W.

NITZ   Lice Infested Crew Necks, $28.75 ppd.

7

Our Bush Jackets

Organic vegetation offers many interesting features to the outdoorsman. It is light in weight, well ventilated, and may rustle in the breeze. These unusual Jackets are made out of fully grown, living plants that have been trimly tailored to Our specifications; root systems tuck conveniently into footwear for easy mobility. Highly prized by peeping Toms, tree worshippers, and topiary fetishists, they are available in 3 models for different uses and weather conditions. Each comes in adequate packing soil and attractive, terra-cotta storage urn. Weight and Height depend.

One size fits all.

The Hunter: Made out of a stand of fresh marsh grass, this good looking, moist Jacket eliminates the need for bulky duck blinds and makes camouflage gear redundant. Move slowly when stalking prey to avoid making squishing noises.

TIPTOE   Hunter Bush Jacket, $119.50 ppd.

The Suburban: This bias-cut privet hedge is correct leisure wear for garden parties, lawn parties, and picnics. Not for wear around pets. Available with square cut or natural shoulders.

P.L.U.   Suburban Bush Jacket, $119.95 ppd.

The Saguaro: For cool comfort in blazing heat, you will enjoy the protection, good looks, and self-contained water supply of this full-grown, succulent cactus. Special care during on-off Recommended. Spiny toggles assure snug fit.

CAREFL   Saguaro Bush Jacket, $119.95 ppd.

Renovated Decoys

Two hand-finished Decoys of imported, high density, heat-processed cork with air-dried white pine heads are mounted on a walnut stained, solid white pine base with attractive natural burlap shade and socket for 100 watt bulb. Waterfowl looking for real estate investments are drawn to Decoys in belief that marsh has gone condo. Wt. 8 lbs.

LEQUAK   Renovated Decoys, $135.00 ppd.
(Insider's price)

Designer Jean

Solid State Jeans

Extremely long-wearing and chic denim Jean designed to Our specifications by Sergio Monadnock. Snug, alluring fit caresses several interesting muscle groups. Two-inch belt loops are 2″ wide to allow plenty of room for unusual belt styles. Metal zip fly works smoothly in all climates and time zones. Jean is pre-washed for comfort, shrinkage control and clingy, second-skin look your date will love. A rugged, durable pant with oodles of panache.

Jean is as suitable for chopping wood in camp as for tooting up in town. Wt. 20 oz.

Color: Soigné Indigo.

Men's and Women's sizes: Waist measurements 28–40, plus, 14, 17, 43, 51, and 54.

Inseams: 31, 32, 33.

OOLALA   Designer Jean, $41.50 ppd.

Innovative trouser incorporates electronic fly system which "zips" up or down when top button is pressed. "Scrubber" chips in brass rivets at stress points make Jeans self-cleaning. Self-fading and self-tailoring, Jeans are Guaranteed to fit like glove and feel great after 27 seconds of wear. These Jeans are worn by United States Astronauts during their leisure time in space.

Color: Futurismo Blue. One size fits anything. Weight, Classified.

O-WOW   Solid State Jeans, $198.25 ppd.

Town Condom

Good-looking velvet Condom is suitable for formal affairs. Medium weight rayon velvet is very absorbent and has thick, soft finish for delightful effects. English fabric is colorfast and presumed impermeable, or at least impeccable. Traditional tailoring with welt seams and silk drawstring fits well on traditionally shaped men. Dry Clean. Wt., 3 oz.

Three colors: Wine. Bottle Green. Black. Monogram Available.

SUAV   Town Condom, $8.50 ppd.
SUAVMOI   Town Condom with Embroidered Monogram
(Three letter maximum in gold thread. Allow 6 weeks for delivery), **$11.00 ppd.**

Ten Speed Racing Socks

Made for Us by State O'Pain, a small company of vegetarian fanatics who jog for fun, these well-made, absorbent, and cushioning socks greatly improve athletic performance and speed. Ninety percent wool with 10% Lectratex™ fabric transmits electric shock to feet in measured increments controlled by handheld rheostat. Provides additional motivation and energy during races or workouts. Snug, rib-knit ankle holds Sock firmly in place; heating wires will not tangle. Not recommended for wear in rain. One size fits all. Wt. ¼ lb. per pair. Color: Grim Grey with Safety orange trim.

KICK   Ten Speed Racing Socks, $11.75 ppd.

Inflatable Ankle Pods

Specially designed for walking on water. Rubberized nylon MiracleSkin™ bladder fills with helium when wet, allowing crossage over deep or troubled waters without heavy equipment. Also useful for holiday pageants, religious fraud, and water ballet. Pods protect ankles from abrasive debris, pollutants, and cooties. One pair of Ankle Pods holds an average-sized man (172¼ lbs.) with an average portage load (57 lbs. plus half a canoe), one small man carrying more than his share, or Robert Morley holding a pound of butter. One size fits all.

DICTU   Inflatable Ankle Pods, $33.33 ppd.

Camouflage Maternity Jumper

Stylish, practical outfit provides good camouflage for expectant outdoorswomen. Breathable Super Chandu cotton is simply tailored with heavy-duty gathers at yoke to allow plenty of room for growth. This versatile frock looks equally well in a duck blind as in an ob-gyn's waiting room.

Three sizes: Sm. Med. Big Mother.

STORK   Camouflage Maternity Jumper, $49.75 ppd.

11

Surgeon's Toque

Doctors who enjoy cooking will appreciate this 100% Sanforized twill Toque decorated with the insignia of the American Medical Association in appliquéed satin with embroidered silk snake. Hat keeps hair out of eyes, dandruff and cold sweat out of incisions and casseroles. Traditional, full blouson styling combines dashing appearance with room for virtually any hair style. Absorbent cotton fabric is useful for wiping soiled or bloody fingers or utensils. Equally at home in kitchen or OR, Our Toque makes a handsome gift for the flashy heart man with a Garland Range or the simple country doctor with a hibachi. Machine Wash. Line Dry.

Four sizes: Plongeur. Saucier. Sous-chef. Chef.

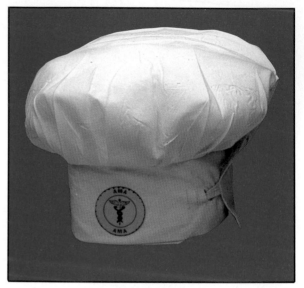

Wt. 5 oz.   Color: Hippocratic Oath White.

CUT   Surgeon's Toque, $9.00 ppd.

Hair Shirt

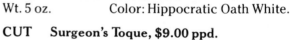

Lightweight, packable discomfort for the outdoor or travelling martyr. Genuine goat hair in patented mesh weave causes painful scratching as effectively as penitential garments of much bulkier design. Shirt is impregnated with a specially formulated fluid which smells bad and burns slightly for weeks. Refills Available. Mortifies flesh and invigorates prayer. Snug, binding fit with drawstring hood and waist provides maximum contact with irritating surfaces. Comes with 2 oz. bottle of Humility Fluid and Our best wishes.

One size befits all.

MOTES   Hair Shirt, $17.25 ppd.

Weight about 6 oz.

Celestial Anorak

A long-wearing gown that is a favorite of angels, seraphs, and deities. Woven of YahwehLon™, a divinely inspired synthetic that is lighter than air, younger than springtime, and impervious to changes in climate, altitude, or ontological status. Cut roomy to fit over a pack for extended visitations or a sweater in case of draft. Trim, incorporeal appearance. Cool enough for wear in outer circles of Inferno. Not for wear in H---. A practical, divine garment that should provide an eternity of wear. Guarantee not valid after Judgment Day. No cleaning Necessary. Wt. one tiniest part of the head of a pin.

Four sizes: Cherub,
                 Angel.
                 Deity.
                 Mr. Big.

Celestial Anorak, $24.95 ppd.

Color: Whiter Shade of Pale.

Turtlehead Shirts

These comfortable Shirts have very full collars which can be pulled up over wearer's face or entire head, affording a convenient, portable redoubt when escape from daily tensions is necessary. Firm interlock fabric is specially treated to absorb cold sweat; its soft finish will not irritate hives, acne, or boils.

Rich, vat-dyed colors resist peekage, although light colors may permit partial see-through in strong light. Shirts are comfortable for active wear, frantic wear, or sitting quite still. An attractive garment with a built-in re-grouping feature, these Shirts are much appreciated by pathologically shy or anxious men and women, and are essential gear for admirers of Bazooka Joe.

Seven colors: Beebleberry. Faded Violet. Overcast Grey. Blanched White. Mortified Red. Cinammon Toast. Crazed Beige.

SHY **Turtlehead Shirt, $12.75 ppd.**

Mr. Goodcuff Jumper Links

Handsome dresswear accessories double as professional quality jumper cables. Miniature heavy-duty, 400 amp ABS clamps keep French cuffs trim and transfer maximum conductivity to battery terminals. Non-chafing, twelve-foot rubber-coated cables fit up sleeves and wrap unobtrusively around torso. Highly recommended for motor trips in cold weather while formally dressed. Wt. 8 lbs. per pair.

+ − + −   Mr. Goodcuff Jumper Links, $19.75 ppd.

Boogie Down Suit

Not an insulated cold weather garment, this colorful, well-designed outfit is suitable for inner city and ghetto wear. Padded shoulders help cushion weight of large portable tape recorders. Flap pockets and rear inverted box pleat protect from rain, wind, and s--- like that. Drape Shape, Stuff Cuff, and handsewn interlinings make for extremely bad, good looks. A tough wearing garment for hard use. Wt. 1½ lbs.

Four sizes: Reet Petite. Dude. Mutha. Big Mutha.
Five Colors: Rusty Funk. Bobby Bland Blue. Eddie Harris Tweed. Black. Camouflage.

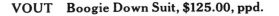

VOUT   Boogie Down Suit, $125.00, ppd.

Beard Guards

High-impact automotive polystyrene Guards for protecting faces of people who kiss or nuzzle hirsute husbands, lovers, or ships that pass in the night. Wraparound ear-pieces keep mask firmly in place, leaving lips and most of face above beard line free for hugs, kisses, and general nookieage. Mask is colorless and blends inconspicuously with most faces. May be trimmed with scissors or glued in place for snug fit. Wipe clean with a damp cloth. Wt. 3 1/13 oz.
GLABRS   Beard Guard, $2.50 ppd.

Fidgeter's Skirt

Women who are on first dates, job interviews, or trying to quit smoking will appreciate this good looking Skirt with many features for frequent adjustment. Wraparound style with overlapping back panel and button waistband permits extensive centering activity, panel straightenage, and button play. Skirt provides 8″ beyond normal waistline for nervous binges or wind. Patch pockets hold all feasible essentials. Fine quality, medium-wale corduroy has neat appearance, is comfortable and able to withstand repeated brushing and smoothing. Weight about 18 oz.
Two lengths: Regular, 26″ from top of waistband. Dowdy, 29″ from top of waistband.
Four colors: Quiet Wheat. Deflated Slate. Queasy Kelly. Polite Navy.
SOTTO   Fidgeter's Skirt, $39.00 ppd.

Tropical weight Pant and Shirt have zip-off arms and legs for brief, strange, or forbidden interludes in warm weather. Pure cotton poplin is light as gossamer and breathable as an angel's lung. Jacket has separate pockets for address book, credit cards, birth control devices, Lip Chaps, rawhide thongs, little tubes of honey, and other light dunnage. Pant has patch pocket, carpenter pocket, butcher pocket, baker pocket, candlestick pocket, Herbert Pocket, and detachable packet pocket. Natural shade hides dirt, stains, and wrinkles well. Washes easily. Dries eventually. Manufactured for Us by Frederick's of Freeport, Our Tropical Quickie Suit is an excellent outfit for strip poker.

Color: Dusty Khaki.

Jacket sizes: Sm. Med. Lg. X-Lg. Please specify sleeve length: Short. Normal. Boarding House.

Pant sizes: Sm.-Med. Med-Lg. Please specify measurements with order.

WAMBAM Tropical Quickie Suit, $52.40 ppd.

Tropical Quickie Suits
(For Men and Women)

Trail Wrap

Made in Portugal for use by Portuguese Army officers and their wives, this handsome shawl is made of cotton strands woven into a loose mesh. Camouflage pattern breaks up line of evening gown or dress uniform, allows revelers to put on dog without frightening animals or alerting guerrillas close by bivouac area. Wrap may be used as scarf, veil, or tourniquet. Traditional Latin workmanship will provide many moments of wear.

Size: 64" x 70". Wt. 8 oz.

LISB Trail Wrap, $9.25 ppd.

—Salinger Cap—

If you really want to know about this item, you probably want to know what it's made out of, and what it's insulated with, and what the goddam *earflaps* are made out of and all that kind of crap but to tell you the truth, that stuff really bores me and anyway, that's not what I want to tell you about this Hat. What I want to tell you about this Hat is about how I got it to be warm and serviceable and all for terri-

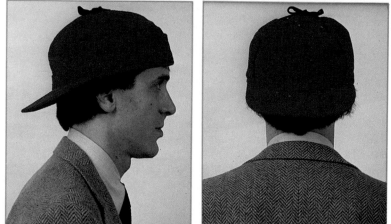

fically cold weather activities just before I got kicked out of prep school at the end of Fall Term. I was feeling pretty crumby when I walked by this Store and there was this terrific Hat right there in the window. I'll tell you what kind of Hat it was. It was made of this tough, mid-wale corduroy that was just like the corduroy on this corduroy shirt my brother had that he was really crazy about the summer before he died. The Hat, the Hat in the Store I mean, was fully rayon-lined and the generous, unbreakable visor's underside was covered in dark green cotton to cut

glare. It had these terrific earflaps that tied under your chin for comfortable protection in extreme cold. It made me feel so damn glad I just started to cry. Right there in the goddamn street. So I bought it and wore it right out of the Store. Suitable for town wear. It really is.

Three colors: Terrifically Red. Kind of Tan. Extremely Green. Three sizes: S-M-L.

JD   Salinger Cap, $8.25 ppd.

Wt. 6 oz.

—Weinberger Cap—

Lightweight insulation while facing down, facing off, or facing facts. Dupont Hollowman II™ polyester Fill and mouton fur-lined eye, ear, and nose flaps prevent dangerous exposure to relevant data, differing opinions, or mortal fear. Adjustable ribbon tie provides snug fit for thorough elimination of foresight, hindsight, or vision; leaves mouth free for threats, smears, and fabrications. Smart, aggressive styling makes any occasion a confrontation.

Two colors: Brawny Beige. Camo.

TUFFY   Weinberger Cap, $19.84 ppd.

18

Chain Mail Hat

An unusual and sturdy free-form Hat that adapts to suit the wearer. Designed by Conan of Katahdin and hand-forged in the rural St. George River Valley of Maine, it is made of 100% iron links for maximum protection from swordsmen, debris, and dragons. Clean and dry carefully to protect from rust. One size fits all.

CLANK   Chain Mail Hat, $38.50 ppd.

Wt. 11 lbs. Color: Iron.

Electric Bonnet

Modern version of traditional Amish headgear. Bonnet is made up of thick-napped, absorbent cotton flannel lined with asbestos for good protection from wiring. Electrical heating system affords comfort and warmth in inclement weather. Bonnet will not pill, sizzle, or melt in case of short circuit. Water resistant when worn with rubber Electric Bonnet Protector (Not included). Plugs into standard AC outlet. Six-inch extension cord allows mobility in a variety of situations. Machine Washable.

75W   Electric Bonnet, $20.50 ppd.
100W   Electric Bonnet Protector, $37.50 ppd.

Three colors: Shocking Pink, Electric Blue. Camouflage.

Child's Excursion Bell and Safety Collar

Copper-plated Bell with loud tone enables parent or guardian to keep track of child in video arcades, shopping malls, or dense cover. Bell is securely anchored to blaze orange nylon Collar with triple-stitched fluorescent reflector strip for good visibility over open ground. "Roll" ring at back of collar makes for easy leash attachment or tieoff. Wt. 6 oz.
Sizes: S, M, L, Husky.

C'MERE   Child's Excursion Bell and Safety Collar, $7.25 ppd.

Country Knee Pads

Handsome Knee Pads covered in 100% cotton duck give comfort and protection in the field, around the yard, in sports and, naturally, at home, cottage, or camp. Thick foam padding protects delicate knees from black-and-blueage. Wide elastic bands hold Pads snug. Covers are Machine Washable. Remove foam to air. Wt. ⅔ lb.
Four patterns: Blue Gingham Check. Red Gingham Check. Madras. Camouflage.
Two sizes: Knobby. Sleek.

ADUB   Country Knee Pads, $6.75 ppd.

20

Summerweight
Dominatrix Ensemble

Good-looking, commanding outfit leaves absolutely no doubt as to who wears pants while remaining breathable and cool. Specially woven nylon stretch breeches have goatskin knee and thigh patches for extra protection while riding, kicking, or humping. Cool crisp, sleeveless blouse has razor sharp Permstarch™ pleats which can actually cut careless, uninvited grabbers or handlers. Good-looking black leather boots have bass-tone heel and toe taps for ominous clickage on hardwood or tile floors. Three feet of bicycle chain Included for use as belt, necklace, or leash. Outfit looks well with Town Quirt.

Three sizes: Little Bitch. Milady. Her.

Uh-O Summerweight Dominatrix Ensemble, $72.75 ppd.

Town Quirt

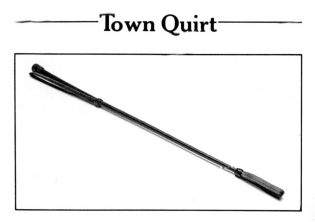

This handy miniature whip is useful for posing threats, emphatic gesturing, or surprising friends. Quirt has strong plastic center for swift flexion and maximum snappage. Covered in handsome pigskin with braided pigskin handle and wrist loop for casually commanding good looks, Our Quirt is a sure attention-getter during tête-à-têtes, business meetings, or family get-togethers. Wt. 9 oz. Length 20¼″.

LARUE   Town Quirt, $19.58 ppd.

Our Weighted Handbags

Tasteful, handy Handbag nicely organizes everday gear while providing discreet self-defense. About 4 lbs. of lead pellets are sewn unobtrusively into Handbag's lining. Adjustable strap allows for powerful swing regardless of sleeve length or upper body strength. Leather reinforcements at wear and impact points. Two zippered compartments, three snap-closing pouches, and four separate inside compartments provide innumerable possibilities for storing keys, wallet, and personal gear. Wt. 4 lbs. 7 oz. Size: 12″ x 7″. Two colors: Don't Mess with Me, Tan. Blackand Blue.

WHAP   Our Weighted Handbag, $15.25 ppd.

Goblin Poncho

Full-length protection for trick-or-treatage in inclement weather. Neoprene-coated nylon Poncho is cut full to fit over costume, booty, and mischief-making apparatus. Drawstring hood protects wigs, crowns, helmets, or horns without ruining everything. Elasticized cuffs and extra-full shoulder-arm construction will not grab or bind when making frightening gestures or saying "Booga-Booga-Booga!" Large front pocket with snap flap holds small candies or Unicef money with ease. Wt. 13 oz.

Two colors: Icky Green. Oocky Brown.

BOO   Goblin Poncho, $10.31, ppd.

"Joggernaut" Electric Feet

These battery-powered Feet can perform many tasks traditionally done by the human variety, including walking, dancing, and smelling. They make excellent training partners for both the casual jogger or serious runner. They are useful for breaking in new shoes, stomping grapes, or holding a place in line. Lonely people may take them dancing; they are very cheap dates. Smaller sizes may be enjoyed by parents of grown children who miss the pitter-patter of little Feet around house, cottage, or camp. Handheld control unit and Stuff Socks Included. Wash Feet frequently, then dust with antifungal powder. Keep warm and dry when not in use. With proper care, these handy Feet should provide miles of service. Wt. 6 lbs. per pair. Whole and half sizes 6–13. No 12½.

Two colors: Feet of Blue. Athlete's Beige.

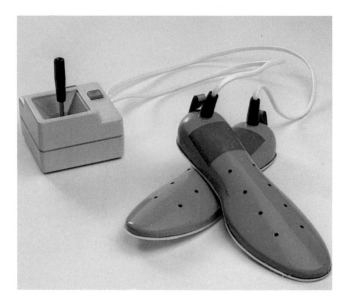

PEDO "Joggernaut" Electric Feet, $22.25 ppd.

Mink Oil

Before applying Mink Oil

After applying Mink Oil

Turns cloth or down coats into sumptuous furs overnight. Boots can be transformed into warm, comfortable mukluks. Shoes become cozy booties. Mink Oil may be used to add fur trim to lapels, pockets, or cuffs. Apply generously with gentle brushing motion for even coat. A much appreciated gift item, Our Mink Oil is an economical yet luxurious way to revitalize a winter wardrobe. Six ounce tin makes one full-length coat, two bolero jackets, or four stoles.

FUH   Mink Oil, $215.25 ppd.

Wt. 5½ lbs.
per boot.

Butch Boot

Juvenile delinquents, former Green Berets, and true believers will enjoy this Boot's awesomely virile appearance. Black, oil-tanned leather, steel shank and Goodyear welt construction protect feet from cold, damp, or weight of Mack Truck rolling over them. Double thick rubber sole by No Skidding™ is Guaranteed to never skid. Spacious, reinforced heel cup holds height enhancers up to 3″. Weight 6 lbs. per boot.

Whole and half sizes: 6–13. No size 9½.

101   Butch Boot, $59.75 ppd.
DEISL Women's Butch Boot.
           Same styling as Our Men's
           Butch Boot. $59.25 ppd.

"Bout du Badoupe"
Insulated Dance Boots
(For Men and Women)

Mukluk-styled Dance Boots from Les Amis Sportifs de Cyd Charisse of Québec, who have been making winterweight dance wear since 1953. Flexible leather bottoms are bonded to slush-proof natural crepe sidewalls for instep protection and arch support *sur pointe*. Polished steel taps are deeply scored for skidless time steps and shuffles on ice. Sueded leather moc-toe uppers, "Ghillie-Tie" lacings and virginal acrylic lining make these Boots ideal for Waltzing, clogging, or shaking tail feather in blizzards, drifts, or tundras.

Men's sizes: 6–12. No half sizes.
Women's sizes: 6½–12½. No whole sizes.

PLIÉ   "Bout du Badoupe" Insulated Dance
              Boot for Men, $59.75 ppd.
RELEVÉ "Bout du Badoupe" Insulated Dance
              Boot for Women, $59.50 ppd.

Wt. 5 lbs. per pair.

Freeport Standers

Not made for walking, running, or movement of any sort, these heavy and well-made shoes should last a lifetime of standing around, sitting around, or lying down for a while. Thick, plantation crepe sole is minutely flexible, making it possible to lean or sway. Shoes may be trudged in for short periods. Capacious two eyelet moc-toe pattern has adjustable rawhide collar lacing. Provides something to do while waiting for other shoes to drop.   Color: Brown to Earth.

Weight,
about 23 lbs. per pair.
Sizes: 6–13, whole & half sizes. No size 10.

CLUNKR   Freeport Standers, $41.75 ppd.

Heavy Duty Evening Pump

Premium quality Evening Pump is designed for years of hard service at formal functions. Classic styling combines short vamp, satin edging, and satin bow with cushion insole, steel shank, steel instep, and steel toe. Provides extra support on receiving lines or in processions. Oil resistant sole will not skid on dropped food or during danceage. Excellent Pump for career diplomats, caterers, or ballroom dancing instructors. Wt. about 5¼ per pair.

THUD   Heavy Duty Evening Pump, $41.75 ppd.

Color:
Correct Black.
Whole and half sizes 6–12. No size 10.

Allagash Galosh

A simple, well-proven design offering all-weather foot protection for stationary people standing on soft ground. Sleeved A-frame front pole provides stability and ease of foot placement. Entry flap ties off around ankle. Nylon walls and taffeta coated wraparound floor protect delicate footwear leathers while letting them breathe. Sides may be guyed out for bulky boots, very wide feet, or gout. Galoshes come with mosquito net ankle bindings, poles, pegs, guylines, seam sealer, and Stuff Sack. Wt. 11 oz. per pair.

Three colors: Environment Green.
Earth Tone.
Camouflage.

WEBLOS   Allagash Galosh, $8.25 ppd.

One size fits all.

Rubber Shot Glass

Industrial strength rubber is highly shock absorbent and completely tasteless. Will not impart flavor to liquors or mixers. Useful for precise measurement of mixed drinks, cocktails, or specialty beverages in camp. Glass holds Internationally Recognized Jigger Measurement, exactly 1½ oz. Wt. 3 oz.

Color: Fatigued Green.

DRNKY   Rubber Shot Glass, $3.75 ppd.

Our Environmental Cassette

We make these tapes for travellers who like to pretend they are where they are not or who are not satisfied by the quality of sound they hear on the trail. May be used to heighten concentration, provide distraction, or beef up disappointing natural audio. Camouflage plastic blends well with nature.

Six Cassettes: Blizzard. Hurricane. Night in the Forest. Night on the A Train. Rush Hour on the A Train. Rush Hour on the A Train During a Simultaneous Blizzard and Hurricane. Wt. 3 oz. per cassette.

CrO_2 Our Environmental Cassette, $6.75 ppd.

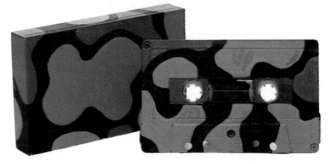

Long-Distance Extension Cord

Power-wind Extension Cord allows use of hair dryer, food processor, and other small electricals up to 5 miles away from home, cottage, or base camp. Steel swing guard for easy feedout of cord over rough or mountainous terrain; ratchet lock prevents automatic retract when far from wall socket. These Cords are a favorite of serious mountaineers and are built to withstand hard use. Handy carry ring for easy tie-off to pack or appliance. Secure plug-in at power source Recommended.

Three Cord lengths: 1 Mile, 3 Miles, 5 Miles.

K2   Long Distance Extension Cord, $43.25 ppd.
(For 1 Mile Model. Add $.10 per 1/7 mile
for 3 and 5 Mile Models.)

Color: Himalayan Yellow.

Musical Utility Boxes

Sturdy, waterproof steel boxes for carrying camera, ammunition, or jewelry while boating or camping. Not "seconds" as are usually found on the market, these Boxes play a tune when the lid is raised. Corrosion resistant finish, welded seams, and rubber gaskets insure long wear and clear, high fidelity tone. Lid is hinged and clamps securely to Box. Will not start playing by accident when stalking prey or lying low.

Color: Jungle Green.

Choice of four tunes: Lara's Theme. Pachelbel Canon. Guys and Dolls. Christmas Medley.

Small Box weighs 4 lbs.

Large Box weighs 6 lbs.

TINKA   Small Musical Utility Box, $12.50 ppd.
TANK   Large Musical Utility Box, $15.75 ppd.

Make-Believe Guitar Strap

Wt. 5 oz.

Popular music fans of all ages will enjoy this soft, top-grain leather Strap which adjusts to fit most guitar surrogates, including broomsticks, umbrellas, ironing boards, and crutches. Frees hands for windmill strums, feverish solos, or easing into splits. Slips off in seconds for storage or if caught unawares in front of mirror. Unobtrusive styling goes with punk, rock, or blues fantasies.

KEITH   Make-Believe Guitar Strap, $21.25 ppd.

Our Pornography

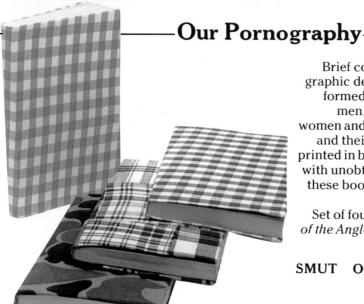

Brief connecting narratives interrupt graphic descriptions of bizarre acts performed by men and women, men and men, women and women, men and women and animals, and men and women and their gear. Titillating effect. Nicely printed in black ink on good quality paper with unobtrusive, stain repellant covers, these books should stand up to years of self-abuse.

Set of four titles: *Bound to Please. Lure of the Angler. Moosehide and Me. Kiss My Chocks.*

SMUT   Our Pornography, $12.50 ppd.

Our Fruit Picker

A favorite of illegal aliens for its durability and comfort, this pack-style fruit basket is specially designed for the migrant farm worker. Carefully handwoven from selected rattan and seasoned white ash, it is correctly shaped to fit the back comfortably, while leaving hands free to climb ladders, pick fruit, or show papers. Equipped with heavy, adjustable webbing harness with sponge rubber pads, Our Picker also provides a safe container for bulky goods such as household belongings or small children. Ideal carryall for riding the rails, hitchhiking, or dodging border guards.

HUELGA   Our Fruit Picker, $30.75 ppd.

Three sizes: Pequeño. Medio. Grande.

Opera Periscope

A boon to the diminutive theatregoer, voyeur, or rush-hour victim. High-resolution optics coated for maximum light transmission produce a bright, crisp image around pillars and over hats, bouffant hair-dos or walls. Die-cast metal barrel and lens housing are built for hard use in second mezzanines, bleachers, and public transport.

Wt. 6 oz.

GAWK   Opera Periscope, $89.50 ppd.

Prefab Monuments

Strong, roomy full-scale Monuments are easy to set up and very stable. External frame of seamless aluminum tubing is barely visible, while shock-corded suspension system absorbs wind stress. Keeps Monument trim. May be used as memorial, camp site or tourist attraction in remote areas. Double closure systems with no-see-um netting at all entrances & windows. Nylon coil zippers will not jam or break during festivals, visiting hours, or observances. Carry sack, poles, stakes, and seam sealer Included. Weight about 396 lbs. 14 oz. per Monument.

Four models: Taj Mahal. Sphinx (with Pyramid vestibule). Grant's Tomb. Uniroyal Tire.

OZY   Prefab Monument, $1,238.75 ppd.

Taj Mahal

Sphinx

Grant's Tomb

Uniroyal Tire

Skiing Chalet

Two-story, three-bedroom house in attractive Swiss Rustic style attaches to four industrial strength touring skis for safe downhill transport in snow. Comes with self-contained heating and plumbing systems and standard 3-pin 75 mm. bindings. Sandbags in corners will provide stability on level ground in winds up to 18 mph or less. Corners lift with ordinary automobile jack for easy ski on— off. Tie-off loop for car, tractor, or skimobile is firmly anchored in exterior chimney wall. House overcomes inertia easily. Waking the family up with a quick *schuss* down the slopes is a traditional Christmas treat in the Swiss Alps. Convenient and economical way to travel during winter months as well. Not for use on conventional chair lifts. Chalet comes unassembled for shipping. Instructions Included. Weight 6,327½ lbs.

Color: Gingerbread with Frou-Frou Trim.

OVALT   Skiing Chalet, $25,000.75 ppd.

Chicken Gun

Developed by the United States Air Force using taxpayers' money, this 12 Gauge Shotgun has been specially adapted to fire dead chickens. Gun is useful for protecting home, surprising friends, testing windshields, or shooting extra-large skeet. Saves ammunition while ridding home, cottage or camp of spare dead chickens. Gun can expel fowl weighing as much as 4 lbs. at speeds approaching 700 m.p.h. Defrost, fold, and truss bird carefully before loading (Instructions Included). Not for use with breaded, unplucked, or boned chickens, or with chicken parts; duck or goose fat may clog firing pin.

Weight 6½ lbs.

WINGY   Chicken Gun, $2,275.25 ppd.

Molotov Cocktails

Made to Our specifications in Londonderry, these professional quality bombs are truly destructive and have undergone numerous tests to prove this. Superior construction of inner and outer walls seals space between, which is filled with glass shards, nails, and lye. Chip-resistant finish for inconspicuous good looks. All-cotton string fuse fits snugly through leak-proof screw-in stopper with nickel plated cap. Thermos-like appearance. These Cocktails are highly prized by terrorists, fanatics, and concerned homeowners. Explosives not included. Not for sale in Continental U.S. or Hawaii any way.

IRA   Pint Molotov Cocktail, $23.75 ppd.
PLO   Quart Molotov Cocktail, $27.50 ppd.

Car Top Heliport

Durable, easy-to-use rack permits three-or four-point landing by most helicoptors. Anodized aluminum cross bars rest on tough, neoprene lined feet, adhere to auto roof with propylene webbing straps and muttered prayers. Rack is not designed to accommodate gunships or troop transports. Landing not recommended when auto is in motion. Stuff Sack Included.

Ten sizes: Mini. Subcompact. Compact. Family Compact. Midsize. Midsize and a Half. Quasi-Fullsize. Fullsize. Luxury. Big Rig Boat. Wt., Equal to the Task.

WHRLY Car Top Heliport, $61.75 ppd.

Electronic Fly Swatter

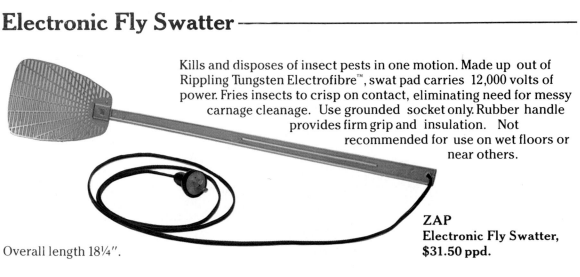

Kills and disposes of insect pests in one motion. Made up out of Rippling Tungsten Electrofibre™, swat pad carries 12,000 volts of power. Fries insects to crisp on contact, eliminating need for messy carnage cleanage. Use grounded socket only. Rubber handle provides firm grip and insulation. Not recommended for use on wet floors or near others.

Overall length 18¼".

**ZAP
Electronic Fly Swatter,
$31.50 ppd.**

Our Spectrahair Kit

Twenty-six preblended, dyed 1 oz. tufts, the complete spectrum of cranial, axial, pubic, and designer shades, is at your fingertips with this Kit. Tufts blend well for accurate match or imaginative contrast with natural hair's color and texture. Provides enormous variety of decorative possibilities for body, wardrobe, or random items. Stuff Sack Included. Wt. 26 oz. Colors: Blonde, Brunette, Redhead, Grey, Silver Midst the Grey, Mousy, Flaxen, Black, Cream, Light Cahill, Mousy Brown, Dark Dunn, Duck Dunn, Olive Dunn, Cinammon Caddis, Shocking Pink, Conventional Pink, Archie Orange, Burnt Orange, Hare's Ear, Dark Hare's Ear, James Brown, Violet at Dawn, Shrimp Boat, Deep Blue, Banana. Comes with 1 oz. jar of Our Dandruff and 2 oz. bottle of spirit gum.

TUFTY   Our Spectrahair Kit, $43.50 ppd.

─────Droll Yankee Goose Duck and Call Bladders─────

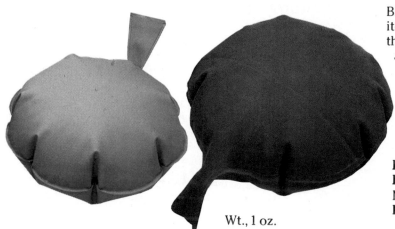

Wt., 1 oz.

Made to Our specifications by Kurt Blooey, who has been crafting amusing items for Us since his parole in 1967, these inflatable rubber Bladders emit authentic bird calls when squeezed or sat on. Though not as loud as Our St. Francis™ Bird Calls, these clever Bladders are handy in case of other-duck-call loss or breakdown, or for pepping up dull parties, trips, or evenings at home.

BLAT   Droll Yankee Duck Call Bladder, $1.75 ppd.
MMPH   Droll Yankee Goose Call Bladder, $1.75 ppd.

Leak Sealant

Our Sealant is popular with many laconic Maine Guides who find it to be an easy-to-use, effective, and long-lasting means of stopping leaks from trusted inner circles and sanctums. Psycho-effective, alum-based compound tightens lips and jaws while reducing blood flow to frontal lobes causing forgetfulness, feeble-mindedness, and paranoid fear of surprise IRS audit. Will not soften resolve of patsies, flunkies, or hit men. Sealant goes on mouth and temples with handy dauber (Included). Eight ounce tin contains enough Sealant to keep an average stooge quiet for four years.

MUM   Leak Sealant, $40.00 ppd.

Tack Shelter

Leather case lined with sheepskin will safely hold up to four dozen thumb tacks, pushpins, or carpet nails. Store pushpins on their sides (Instructions Included). Two pockets behind sheepskin hold needles, pins, favorite cookie fortunes, or bits of string. Fits easily into pocket or pack. Velcro closure keeps Shelter closed, preventing accidents. Convenient way to carry tiny, pointy gear. Size, 3½″ x 8″. Wt. 4 oz.
Color: Tacky Brown.

TIC   Tack Shelter, $14.00 ppd.

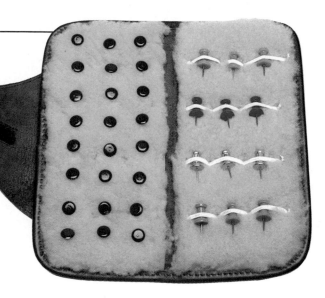

Our Hiking Cue

This combination walking stick and billiard Cue meets a wide range of functional requirements and has proven a favorite of itinerant or sporting hustlers, con artists, and suckers. Solid walnut shaft is finished with a braided pattern for sure grip while navigating rough terrain or applying heavy English. Nylon webbing wrist thong is helpful during break shots or in case of trippage. Screw-off brass cap protects leather cue lip from pavement and dirt. Comes with three Cue tips and Booklet explaining enough about Straight Rail Billiards, 3-Rail Billiards, and Snooker to intimidate anyone who does not actually play them.

J.T.S.   Our Hiking Cue, $43.21 ppd.

Three lengths: 48″. 54″. 60″.
Wt. 19, 21, or 23 oz.

Watt-Me-Worry™ Environmental Gear

These products are designed and built by Dr. Alfred E. Watt, whose bold field experiments have secured a reputation not only as an environmentalist, but as a pioneer of modern autoproctology. Each provides easy management of natural inconveniences caused by earth, wind, sky, animals, plants, or excessively poor people. Each is hand-crafted from non-biodegradable materials that are Guaranteed to last and last and last. Significant corporate discounts available on these items.

Home Defoliant

A good spraying with this Defoliant can transform 600 square feet of lawn, garden, or brush into a dust bowl within minutes. Protects home and property from overgrown foliage and dangerous animal life while preparing land for further development. Forty-eight hour evacuation after use recommended. Insect mutations and future medical costs not covered by Our Guarantee. Two gallons of Defoliant come nicely put up in metal tin with adjustable pump spray nozzle which is guaranteed not to damage the ozone layer with fluorocarbons.

GOBI   Home Defoliant, $16.00 ppd.

Ultrasonic Pest Offputter

Effective without poisons or chemicals, this innovative device emits an ultrasonic beam which, though not perceivable by humans or most pets, is so offensive to flying, crawling, or larval insects that they will vacate the premises immediately after installation, taking with them all their personal effects. Offputter has two settings. At Low, suitable for mild infestations, Offputter says simply horrid things to bugs. At High, suitable for plagues, Offputter performs ultrasonic Wayne Newton medley. Unit operates on standard household current and is effective over an area of 2,500 cubic feet. With optional Converter, Offputter is effective on human pests as well. Measures 3¼" x 3¼" x 4½".

BLOW   Ultrasonic Pest Offputter, $23.25 ppd.
SCOOT   Ultrasonic Guest Offputter, $65.25 ppd.

Respirator Mask

Allows easy breathing under a wide variety of contemporary atmospheric conditions. Government Approved design filters out harmful exhaust fumes, cigarette smoke, industrial smog, oiled dust, acid rain, tainted mist, fetid spray, sooty vapor, and toxic substances in general. Durable, contoured face piece with adjustable strap is light enough for constant use, fits comfortably while eating, working, driving, relaxing, wearing glasses, sleeping, or dying.

WHEEZ   Respirator Mask, $19.84 ppd.

Wt. ½ lb.

37

Field Litter Pan

Lightweight, plastic Litter Pan allows cat to maintain proper toilet habits on the trail or in camp. Holds 3 lbs. of deodorized, ordinary, or funky litter granules. Snug lid clamps shut for neatness in pack. Easily washable.

Color: Pale Fawn. Measures 18″ x 12″ x 3″, Wt., ½ lb. (empty).

TUPP   Field Litter Pan, $7.25 ppd.

Aquatic Cat Clothes (And Gear)

Water sports plan an essential role in the physical program of any feline. We make these amphibian aids for the beginning, intermediate, or advanced diving cat or kitten. Paw Fins are made out of a very high grade of rubber that is not only gnaw-proof, but strong enough to give most cats the propulsion they need to dog-paddle properly. Muzzle Mask fits sizes Kitty through Puma without binding, for clear vision in fresh or salt water. The Jellicle Snorkel™ has a fixed elbow design and is sized properly for feline lungs. The Safety Donut is a useful training aid as well as essential gear for white water kayaking. Our Fishcoys™ are life-like cork replicas of little silver fish. Dragged along floor or ground at home, cottage, or camp, they should distract most sportscats long enough for pet owner to eat in peace. Complete set of Clothes and Gear weighs about 3 lbs.

CARL   Aquatic Cat Clothes (And Gear), $51.97 ppd.

Colonial Litter Pan

Hand-fashioned from hardwood with a maple finish, Pan is an authentic replica of an 18th Century design. Bevelled corners will not snag or ruffle fur while claw-and-ball feet provide interest. Graceful lines are conveniently proportioned for all but smallest kittens. Holds up to 4 lbs. of litter material. Clean daily for best care of finish. Pan measures 24″ x 16″. Weighs 8 lbs.

PEW   Colonial Litter Pan, $17.76 ppd.

"Sac du Chat" Cat Panniers

Wt. 26 oz.

Superior quality dual pack for the mountaineering feline. Panniers are useful for carrying bulky gear such as ice axe, litter stores, and liver bits in cream sauce. Zip allows access to small items such as compass, first aid kit, and spare collar. Toggle pulls for easy grip with teeth or paws. Panniers ride low and snug for comfortable, well-balanced fit on the trail, around town, or drowsing on the window sill.

**PURR   "Sac du Chat"
Cat Panniers, $32.25 ppd.**

Aluminum Balalaika Case

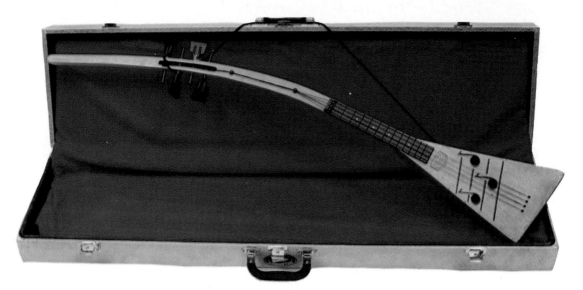

Highly prized by hard-travelling gypsies, *klezmer* musicians, and Soviet diplomats, this professional quality Balalaika Case has a hand-fitted, velvet-lined balalaika-shaped interior, triple-locking, pick-proof hardware, and overlapping side seam insulation for water and shock resistance. Grain embossed, anodized finish looks trim and discourages rust. Case provides optimum conditions for balalaika storage and transport. Violin and Guitar models Available by special order. Wt. 10 lbs., 3 oz.

PLNK   Aluminum Balalaika Case, $92.75 ppd.

Folding Midget's Chair

Very popular on the subcontinent and with children, this comfortable, low-slung Chair is designed for midgets, dwarves, and elves. Strong 1″ aluminum alloy tubing with heavy duck seat and back provide stable seat at low altitude. Enables short people to keep both feet on the ground while taking a load off them. Chair collapses and folds easily for storage or humorous japes.

Two colors: Leprechaun Green. Little Boy Blue.

wee   Folding Midget's Chair, $35.25 ppd.

Wt. 2 lbs. 2 oz.

——"Find-the-Function"——
Wrist Information Center

State-of-the-art wrist tool provides so much data in such a tiny format that it is impossible to use without the Instruction Manual (Included) and a magnifying glass (Not included). In addition to telling time in all time zones, Center's functions include a stopwatch (accurate to 1/zillionth of a second), optional hourly chime, 24 hour alarm, alarum, alarum and excursion, exterior temperature (fahrenheit and centigrade), body temperature (rectal and oral), electroencephalogram, electrocardiogram, current D.&B. rating (if any), plasma glucose level, lymphocyte count, pulse rate, your weight and fortune. Also contains exciting wrist video game for dull moments. Recommended for use with Our Traditional Wrist Watch. Weight, an ounce or 2. Color, Junky Gold or Cheap Silver.

LED[2] **"Find-the-Function" Wrist Information Center, $175.25 ppd.**

British Beach Duo

Made for Us by Brenda of Blackpool, Ltd., this versatile Hat and Shirt Duo is a favorite of many professional life guards, surfers, and pearl divers who work Great Britain's beaches. The casual, singlet-style Shirt is lightweight and cool when worn by itself, while its patented, "fishnet" weave traps warm air next to the skin when worn under a shell or a cardigan; prevents chill in case of sudden nippy spells or unexpected cloudage. Hat keeps glare off head while keeping hair and scalp trim and draft-free. Knots adjust for custom fit or untie completely, permitting use of Hat as handkerchief (Instructions Included). Also functional for spectator sports, gardening, or enjoying a nice cup of tea in the open air, the British Beach Duo is highly prized by the outdoorsman who finds the sun setting on his vacation more than he'd anticipated. Made of fine, sea island cotton, the Duo is Machine Washable, up to a point. Line Dry, if you please. Duo comes with a 2 oz. tube of Our Zinc Oxide to prevent nose burn, and a 4 oz. disposable thermos flask of English Breakfast Tea. Four sizes: Little Chappie. Good Fellow. Stout Fellow. Bloody Great Bloke.

'LO,LUV **British Beach Duo, $12.15 ppd.**

Our Questionnaire

Please help Us to serve you better by answering these questions, honestly and truly, to the best of your knowledge and ability, cross your heart and hope to die. Use as much time as you need; don't stint. Use extra paper (Not included) for additional comments. Show finished questionnaire to friends, hide in shame, bake in pie, stick in eye, shred, keep, eat or throw out as desired. Please do not mail it to Us. You may begin now.

1) What is your age? _____

2) What is your age, *really?* _____

3) Sex: Male _____ Female _____ Other (Please be specific) _____

4) Marital Status: Solid _____ Complacent _____ Troubled _____ Working on It _____ On the Rocks _____ Free to Be You and Me _____

5) Education: Some high school _____ High school _____ Some college _____ Which one? _____ Clubs, distinctions, teams, degrees _____

6) Income: Under $10,000 _____ Under $25,000 _____ Under $40,000 _____ Under $75,000 _____ Over $100,000 _____*

7) Occupation: Business (sales, marketing, textiles, buttons, etc.) _____ Professional (teacher, lawyer, doctor, doctor-a-dentist) _____ Tinker (Pots, pans, oddments repaired) _____ Criminal (Drugs, prostitution, divorce law, real estate, politics) _____ Entertainment (Actor, musician, athlete, dancer, *jongleur*) _____ Homemaker _____ Homewrecker _____ Student _____ Retired _____ Retiring _____ Just very shy _____ Potter _____ Weaver _____ Rainmaker _____ Astronaut _____ Other (Please do not explain) _____

8) How do you pay for your purchases from Our Store? Charge _____ Check _____ Barter _____ Just another deadbeat _____

9) What is your Zip Code _____ Apartment or P.O. Box number _____ How much room do you have? _____ What are you paying? _____ Do you know of any good apartments in Manhattan that aren't too expensive? _____

10) Is there anything you would like to order from Our new Catalog _____ Why not? _____

11) Do you purchase most of your outdoor, indoor and otherdoor items from Us _____ Why not? _____

12) Please list the other mail order stores from which you purchase items. Be thorough: _____
_____
_____ Memorize this list; be sure not to buy from these stores in future.

13) How do you feel about the quality of the products and service you receive from Us?: Fabulous _____ Ecstatic _____ Divine _____ Divoon _____ Warm Glow from Deep Down Inside _____ Tops in Taps _____ Other (Please do not explain) _____

14) Are you a contributor to Our Research and Development Fund? _____ Why not, don't you care? _____

15) What suggestions do you have to improve Our items, service, product inventory, and overall quality (Please limit comments to space provided) _____

Stop. Put down your pencils. Do not turn the page. You have completed this part of Our Catalog. Please keep completed Questionnaire tightly closed in a cool dry place at home, cottage, vault, or camp. Thank you for your help.

---

*If your income exceeds $100,000 a year, please send Us your home phone number and hours when you may be reached. We have important news for you. Act now.

DEAR OUR STORE
letters from Our customers

• I am simply amazed at the consideration and sensitivity Your Staff shows to the average customer. Not long ago I was feeling pretty blue and decided to end it all. I called You guys up to buy a Portable Tombstone so's I could save my people the trouble and expense of doing a whole funeral thing. Dead is dead, who needs it, am I right? Well, I hadn't even finished giving Your operator my order, when she suddenly said, "Hang on, please!" and hung up on me. I was amazed. How did she know? How *could* she know, much less *care*? Well, something inside of me changed then, and I guess you could say I've been hanging on ever since. I just wanted to say thank You. By the way, could I possibly prevail upon You to put in an order for a couple of medium-sized Flannel Shirts, one blue, one red, where it'll get taken care of? I'm enclosing a check. Thanks a heap. Mucho Blessings on You,

—Billy G. Cracker, Spitville, Mo.

• I am a reclusive bachelor who teaches here at our local grade school. For the past three years I have called up and ordered one item a month from Our Store, and returned it the next; I enjoy the conversation. The unfailing promptness and courtesy of Your Staff, not to mention the devilish packing methods You devise to protect your wares en route, have enlivened my spare time considerably.

I've enjoyed chatting several times with one young lady in particular who works in Your Customer Service Department. She has a soft voice with a very slight lisp and she didn't get mad at me when I returned a hat I'd already bought four times in seven months. Do you think you could send me her name and address? I'd like to thank her for her prompt and courteous service with a dried flower arrangement I've made from flowers I grew in my window box. I assure you I'll tear up the information as soon as I've sent the package off. Our Store has been a Godsend for me. Your whole Store's attitude to Your customers is unique. I hope You will post my address on Your bulletin board along with a standing invitation to anyone from Our Store to drop by for tea if They're ever in my neighborhood.

—W. Biddlebaum, Winesburg, Ohio

• What can I say? Beautiful concept, beautiful execution, beautiful prompt and courteous service. I love the stuff I get from Our Store, You hear me? I LOVE IT!
Call me when You're out here, we'll have lunch.

—Lance Momzer, Hollywood, Cal.

• Last week I am sitting on the porch of my little house reading, as is my wont, Spinoza, when suddenly who should appear before my startled peepers but three personalities wearing slouch hats and dark glasses and, most importantly and distressingly, carrying gats. In the melée which ensues, which I am delighted to tell you I survive, I have cause many times to thank my lucky stars that I am wearing my Norwegian Bulletproof Sweater, without which I would right now be one air-conditioned stiff. You Our Store guys are the berries. I owe You.

—Big Julius, Chi-Town, Ill.

• Recently I had occasion to place a mail order with Our Store for a camping trip I was planning. I had just selected the colors, sizes, and other particulars of the items I wanted when suddenly, there was a knock at the door. It was a UPS man, delivering a package from You containing precisely the items I'd just decided to order. I am very curious to know how You were able to do this. I would also like to thank You for Your prompt and courteous service.

—Twyla Zone, Middlebrow, Vt.

Brain Truss

Highly motivated or relentlessly ambitious people will appreciate this lightweight headgear which provides support and relaxation for drained, strained, or overtrained brains. Porous cotton mesh allows scalp to breathe while keeping lid on; thoughts can draft without loss of mind. Conservative, skullcap-type styling makes Truss suitable for office wear, dress code permitting (Not covered by Our Guarantee). Will not block vision or muss hair even after long use. Highly Recommended for final exams, heated negotiations, or standard 70 hour work week. Color, Meshy Beige.

TYP-A   Brain Truss, $9.75 ppd.

Wt. 3 oz.

Tasselled Antennae

Tasteful, idiotic headgear for fraternity parties, drunken sprees, or business school interviews. Strong, long, wiggly springs are topped with rich, hand-rubbed leather tassels which have been rolled and stapled according to traditional patterns. Goes with many contemporary shoe styles. Antennae give advance warning of low-hanging door jamb or fast approaching floor to wearer sober enough to notice. Wt. 5 oz. Color, Rich Brown w/Jolly Metal Trim.

YAHA   Tasselled Antennae, $8.25 ppd.

Down East Roach Traps

Traditional tools of New England exterminators, these Roach Traps are handmade for Us by Claude Horribly of Langouste Cove, Maine, master trap-maker for over 18 months. Sill-trap design with steamed oak bows and hand-knitted, tarred marline twine netting is effective on German roaches, brown roaches, and water bugs up to 2¼". Linseed oil finish brings out attractive grain of laths. Traps fit unobtrusively in corners and under furniture, or may be wall-mounted for handsome seafood-restaurant-like appearance. Traps are easily emptied when full. Each Trap measures 3½" x 1¾" x 1¾" high. Set of 2 Traps weighs 1/6 lb. Four yards marline twine, 2 steel knitting needles for repairs, and Trap-Setting Guide Included.

CRITRZ   Down East Roach Traps, $43.25 ppd.

Color: Well-Worn Wood.

Olde Canterbury Serving Caske

Whan that Aprille with shoures soote,
Hath perced to the lining of yer Aulde Gyde Boote,
Than will ye liken this handye Caske,
Sewtabyl for divers bevryges like sacke.
More comely and dewrable a Caske, swere We,   5
Have We never yseen, by Oure Gauwrantee.
Thyse ilke Caske be maken of oaken staves,
I'fayth, With ye polyurethane coatynge, to staith
Lykyge, and bring oute the comely wooden grayne.
To cleenen thyse Caske, its shyne to retayne,   10
Wyp't with a sponge that's wete but not soppen.
We plight Our troth that thyse Caske will becomen
A parfit, gentil addit'n to home, campe, or jauntes
To ferne halwes, couthe in sondry londes.

Wt. 1 Stone. Holds ⅛ Hogshead.
Color: Vowel Shift Brown.

GEOFF   Olde Canterbury Serving Caske, $140.00 ppd.

Money Changers

Long a favorite of bus drivers, news agents, and pushcart operators, these high quality stainless steel Changers have become popular with employers and parents. Fully loaded Changer holds a week's net take-home pay for all income levels up to 50% tax bracket. Keeps funds close by for use at requisite intervals. Changer attaches easily to belt and is virtually invisible under a buttoned coat or jacket.

Four barrels: 1 Quarter, 1 Dime, 2 Nickel. Wt. about 10 oz. (Empty).

Two styles: With rubber bumper to discourage assaults on coin release levers. Without rubber bumper for dress wear.

¢   **Money Changer, $23.75 ppd.**

Geodesic Dreidel

Traditional Hanukah top is contructed in innovative shape to withstand hard spinnage during holiday season. Made of balsawood struts with tough nylon skin, this lightweight and amusing toy can be disassembled and packed small in seconds for storage or transport. Popular item with the Israeli army. Stuff Sack, assembly and game Instructions Included. Wt. 1/18 lb.

וגהש   **Geodesic Dreidel, $1.75 ppd.**

Weatherproof Breviary

Full texts of all canonical hours are clearly printed on spiral-bound, plastic laminate pages to allow recitation of Divine Offices under a wide variety of conditions. Designed for Us by Father Ham Berrigan, who has incorporated many features based on his experiences in radical safe houses, prisons, lecture halls, and occasionally church. Pages will not fade, crack, or mildew from devotions in severest weather. Illustrations and printing are handsome, inspiring, and fade-proof. Fiberglass reinforced cover keeps pages trim. Thoughtful and divine Christmas gift for hermits, missionaries, or sporting clerics. Wt. .33 lb.

HEURES   Weatherproof Breviary, $25.12 ppd.

Great Bladesmen Pocket Swords

Highly skilled craftsmen from Stiletto Mountain, New Hampshire combine quality materials, superior construction, and adolescent fascinations with violence and weaponry to produce these handsome knives. Suitable for desk-top display or pocket flauntage, each has a laminated hardwood handle with scrimshaw-type inlaid medallion depicting a distinguished bladesman. Each Pocket Sword comes with a certificate signed by the artisan who made it, along with his or her photograph, telephone number, and brief statement of interests and goals. Two-and-a-half inch saberclip blade is sturdy and reliable for light work such as cutting string, trimming nails, or excavating wax-embedded candle wicks. Knives measure 3½″ closed and weigh 4¼ oz.

Four Bladesmen: D'Artagnan. Vlad the Impaler. Basil Rathbone. Norman Mailer.

B'LASTRA   Great Bladesmen Pocket Sword, $35.75 ppd.

Crystal Ball

Traditional Balkan means of predicting future, revealing past, and speaking to dead. Rumanian-made Ball gives clear vision of what is to come and what has been. Wipes clean with a damp cloth for long life. Each Ball is numbered and signed by the warlock who made it. Chamois Stuff Sack Included. Guaranteed for years of rough seanceage. Wt., As Desired. Diameter, 8″.

E.S.P.   Crystal Ball, $133.77 ppd.

Artificial Emergency Dressing

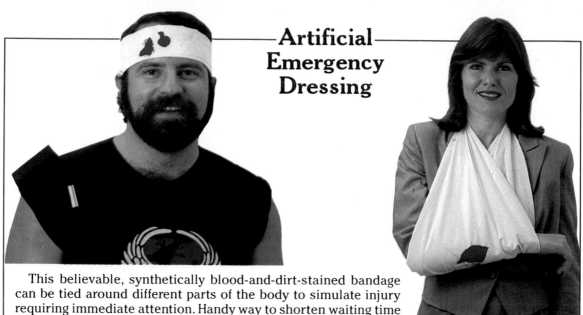

This believable, synthetically blood-and-dirt-stained bandage can be tied around different parts of the body to simulate injury requiring immediate attention. Handy way to shorten waiting time in doctor's office, emergency room, or Friday afternoons at work. Smooth-finish, percale cotton Dressing has smartly frayed edges for urgent, improvised appearance. HolloThrill™ stuffing adjusts easily to resemble broken bone, painful swelling, or stump. Machine wash. Dry in Private. Guaranteed Sympathetic.

COUVAD **Artificial Emergency Dressing, $15.25 ppd.**   Weight, 2 lbs., 3 oz.

Christmas Tree Ornaments

These droll miniature items make handsome Ornaments on most Christmas trees. Well constructed out of fabric, metal, wood, and glue, each is fitted with a tiny hook for firm grip on spruce, fir, or artificial tree branches. Each makes a warm light-weight addition to holiday décor as well as a friendly, subliminal reminder of Us. We recommend hanging several on your tree for long-wearing, festive good looks. Hanging Instructions Included.

Set of 5 Ornaments: Gargantua Boot. Early Warning Tie Tack. St. Francis Design Bird Call. Alice B. Toklas Trail Mix. Brunch Fly. Weight 1.2 lbs.

HOHOHO **Christmas Tree Ornaments, $12.25 ppd.**   Holiday Stuff Sack Included.

Invisible Chin Support

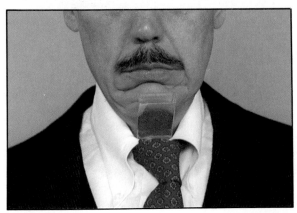

Clear, lightweight plexiglass chin shelf slips under shirt or jacket to hold head up. Aids in appearance of concentration while drifting off at desk, lunch, or meeting. Eliminates head loll or sleepy droolage during office hours.

HM?   Invisible Chin Support, $8.50 ppd.

Wt. 8 oz.

Gift Assemblage Set

Well-wrapped gifts are a traditional sign of esteem, good taste, and breeding. This Set contains all items necessary for handsome, neat gift wrappage: Twenty sheets of Our Gift Wrap in four patterns (Our Logo; Lot O'Ducks; Lot O'Chickens; Camouflage); ten-yard rolls of ribbon, tissue paper, string, cord, and twine; four bows (pre-tied); one bunch of paper flowers in assorted colors; 3 oz. packet of gold foil stars; 84-page Instruction Manual. Makes high quality gift presentation a distinct possibility even for the most butterfingered sportsman.

FORME!?
Gift Assemblage Set,
$14.25 ppd.

Wt. 3 lbs. 4 oz.

Branding Iron

Solid bronze Branding Iron with choice of three initials. Allows simple, one-step identification of wooden possessions, meat stores, or flesh and blood. Handle is polished hardwood with a bronze ferrule and sure-grip finish. Heat over open flame until glowing, then press firmly to desired surface. Not for use on non-consenting adults or minors. Please print initials clearly with order. Wt. 2 lbs. 2 oz.

SSSSS   Branding Iron, $9.50 ppd.

Throw Rug

This Rug may be used as a picnic blanket, decorative floor accent, or as object of exciting games of catch. Tight, braid-weave construction rides wind well for maximum loft and carry. Smooth finish cotton bunting cloth will not snag or fray, enhancing appearance, smooth flight, and sure control on placement shots. Hand-loomed in Scotland where carpets have been tossed for centuries, this handsome item is the versatile ancestor of the modern Frisbee. Diameter, 36″. Weight, 1/3 Stone.

Two colors: Thistle Heather Mix. Unblended Malt Mix.

BRAW   Throw Rug, $26.25 ppd.

Two-In-One Pencil

Air-dried, white pine Pencil with machine centered graphite writing element produces clear lines and can also correct its own mistakes. Red rubber eraser pad removes unwanted markings by means of simple rubbing motion. Six-sided cylindrical shape feels good in hand. Solid brass fittings hold eraser in place. Instructions for point maintenance Included. Length unsharpened, 7 ¼″. Diameter ¼″.
Wt. ¿Quien Sabe?
Two colors: Traditional Yellow Enamel. Camouflage.
SKRCH   Two-In-One Pencil, $.15 ppd.

Droll Yankee Sandwich Sign

An authentic piece of New England folk art recreated by Us, this Sign is similar to signs hung in grocery stores and Italian carryouts throughout Our region. Depicts local slang for hero sandwich, hoagie, grinder, po'boy, sub, torpedo, wedge, or weck. May be used at home, cottage, or camp as witless *double entendre,* crude ethnic slur, or handsome bric-a-brac. One-piece construction with no moving parts, Sign is made of 100% Wood with durable enamel finish. Attaches easily with hook or chain (Neither Included).
Guaranteed Amusing.

Ban-The-Smile Button

Publicizes desire to avoid pointless pleasantries, chitchat, and drivel. Promotes sincerity and directness in private life as well as daily businessage. Trim metal button is standard button shape with triple acrylic finish and traditional, difficult-to-work pin assemblage. Diameter, 1½″. Wt. 3/7 oz.
Color: Unnaturally Sunny Yellow with Basically Black.

GOWAY   Ban-the-Smile Button, $1.025 ppd.

Wt. 1-23/75 lb.

ME.   Droll Yankee Sandwich Sign, $14.25 ppd.

51

Bitch Towel

Thick, pure cotton Towel is decorated with negative and nasty remarks in handsome jacquard weave lettering. Discourages direct approach or contact. Useful tool for creating animosity, distance, or aloof appeal at beach, poolside, or home. Dobby Border prevents frayage. Measures 60″ x 36″.

RUSE   Bitch Towel, $9.75 ppd.

Wt. 2 lbs.
Color: White with Mean Green lettering.

Celtic Legend Dish Towels

These high quality, extremely absorbent, and very entertaining Towels are handsomely imprinted with authentic tales from the vast world of Celtic folklore. Each contains 1 riveting story, suitable for family enjoyment while clearing table or drying dishes, or for personal amusement while performing solitary toweling jobs around home, cottage, or camp. Made of a blend of 86% cotton and 14% thatch, Dish Towels are made for Us in County Connemara by Spórt an Ghrá Soithí na Tuáille, Ltd., longtime suppliers of towels to hotels, hospitals, and tea rooms. Legends are hand silkscreened with vegetable-based pigments that will not run, fade, or discolor unless moistened. Towels' smart appearance makes them suitable for wear as scarves.

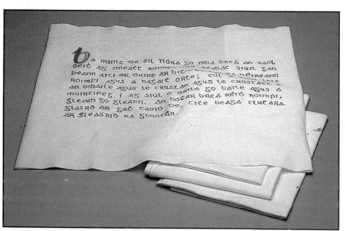

One size: Standard Dish.
Set of 4 Towels contains 1 Irish, 1 Scottish, 1 Welsh, and 1 Basque legend per set: *The Ghostly Shillelagh; The Magical Haggis; The Spirit in the Leek; The Enchanted Beret.*

Wt., 5 oz.

GAELS   Celtic Legend Dish Towels, $13.25 ppd.

Our Georgia Scrapwood

Our Scrapwood is made from specially selected sweepings, discards, and throwouts from Our Workrooms. Some pieces have rusty nails, old paint, or bits of mysterious hardware affixed; many are well splintered, and several are from Georgia. No two are exactly alike. Two or 3 sticks placed in stove or fireplace may ignite quickly and burn with a good flame long enough to start larger logs. On other hand, sticks may lie there smoldering until kindling is added or sputtering flame dies out altogether. A very profitable item for Our Store, We recommend Our Scrapwood as much for the excitement it brings to fire-starting situations as for the added space its absence brings to Our Warehouse. Eleven ¼ lbs. of Scrapwood come packed in good-looking burlap sack for safe handling. Wear gloves to pick out individual pieces.

JUNQ   Our Georgia Scrapwood, $14.25 ppd.

Maps

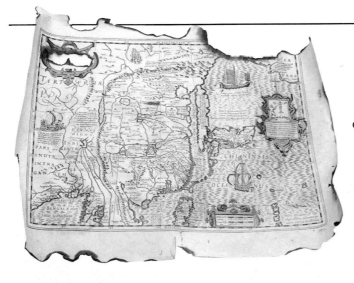

Color: Parchment.

These antique Maps are hand-drawn on well-preserved parchment and feature inscrutable penmanship, bizarre geography, quaint language, and disturbing threats. Each leads to a buried treasure. Booty includes bullion, doubloons, piastres, wampum, jewelry, spices, and blue chip stock certificates. No two are exactly alike. Maps are Guaranteed to provide owner riches beyond avarice or dreams. Please print address and zip code clearly on order form to insure Map will lead to treasure convenient to home, cottage, or camp. Wt. approximately 6 oz. per Map.

Usual measurements about 16″ x 15″.

☠   MAP $150.25 ppd.

53

Clamshell Castanets

Long popular with many of New England's Flamenco, shake, and belly dancers, these genuine quahog Clamshell Castanets are reinforced at the hinge with fiberglass and rubber, then blast-varnished for beauty, scratch resistance, and sonority of tone. Each is individually tuned for optimum volume and click response. Hand-painted trim and colorful tasselling give Castanets a sporty look. Stuff Sack Included.

Wt., about 5 oz. per pair.

OLÉ   Clamshell Castanets, $16.08 ppd.

Hors D'Oeuvres Kit

Handy 10-piece utensil kit designed for general use at cocktail parties, happy hours, and big affairs. Particularly useful when only toothpicks have been provided for buffet; can be used at mealtime as well. Includes Pie Server, Knife, Cheese Plane, Lobster Claw/Nut Cracker, Bottle Opener/Corkscrew, Salt Shaker, Pepper Mill, Swizzle Stick, Napkin, and Analgesic. Inside pocket holds insurance policy and doctor's phone number. Zippered vinyl carrying case with belt clip lies flat for use as tray.   Wt. 1½ lbs.

ESS   Hors D'Oeuvres Kit, $14.75 ppd.

Radar Knife

Beautifully balanced, stainless steel Knife has short-range radar detection system built into handle. Warns carver of approaching bones, sinew, and gristle with soft beep. Reduces confusion and frustration when carving legs of lamb, turkey, or rib roasts. Small model may be used for filleting fish or deboning ortolans. Full tang, fine ground blade attaches to detection circuits in handle with solid brass rivets. Sensitive receiving dish serves as protective hilt. Natural juices will not interfere with transmission. Unit is fully immersible for easy washing. Turn off when slicing bread or meat loaves for prolonged battery life.

Two sizes: 9″ Carver. 3″ Parer.

SNICKER   9″ Radar Carving Knife, $109.75 ppd.
SNEE   3″ Radar Paring Knife, $82.50 ppd.

Bird Seed Pâté

This vegetarian Pâté will attract the most un-usual and finicky birds to your feeder. Good quality seed feed is layered, seasoned, and baked in slow ovens to bring out the distinct flavor of each ingredient. No hulls or red millet are ever used. A slice of this Paté in feeder, garnished with a few sprigs of watercress and perhaps a few capers, should bring in My Little Chickadees, Only-Birds-in-Gilded-Cages, Oiseaux-Lyres, Nervous Titters, and Cardinal Spellman.

Wt. 1 lb. per portion.

DDL   Bird Seed Pâté, $8.25 ppd.

Heavy Duty Cruets

Leak-proof Cruets keep oil and vinegar safe under rough conditions. High density propylene is tasteless and odorless, so subtle flavors of first pressing extra-virgin olive oil or fruit vinegars will not be affected in the field. An essential item for high quality outdoor salads, Cruets are Guaranteed to keep dressings *delizioso.* Wt. 3 oz. per pair. Capacity 4 oz. per Cruet. Our Vinaigrette Recipe Included. Special Herbs not Included.

3/1 Heavy Duty Cruets, $6.25 ppd.
3/1+? Our Vinaigrette Herb Packets,
Six 1 oz. Packets, $3.25 ppd.

Suction Egg Cup

Non-toxic, non-flammable, washable plastic Egg Cup has textured surface for full suction on shell and table. Eliminates motion when eating or serving eggs. Liquid yolks will not swirl. Moisten base and press down firmly to keep Egg Cup in place. Not for use on tablecloths. Useful item for eating breakfast during storms, small quakes, or hangovers. One of Our most popular items with Californians. Holds eggs sized PeeWee to Jumbo.

OVO Suction Egg Cup, $2.25 ppd.

Two colors:
White.
Eggshell.

Haggis Making Kit

Haggis, the National Dish of Scotland, is a stuffed and boiled sheep's stomach. Our easy to use Kit produces a high quality Haggis to suit own taste or dumbfound friends. Blend special seasonings (included) with utility cuts from sheep, lambs, or ewes. Drink Scotch while preparing, eating, and later, when attempting digestion. Kit comes complete with detailed instructions, recipes, sheep's stomach, casing ties, oatmeal, modern cure salts, Rubber Shot Glass, and motion discomfort container for first timers. Leftovers are delicious fried or make up easily into handsome lamp base or insulation strips for window and door frames.
Wt. 14 oz.

H'LOO Haggis Making Kit, $10.31 ppd.

Microwave Televoven
(By VideoBake)

Prepares food in minutes, as well as receiving television broadcasts with life-like clarity. Three-gun, quartz-tuned ColorWow™ visual enhancement system provides vivid picture with razor-sharp definition as well as scrumptious, mouth-watering-in-appearance roasts, stews, and desserts. Automatic timer assures programs will not be missed nor food overcooked. Continuous cleaning interior has ¾ cubic foot cooking capacity, big enough for several full-size food portions. Removable rack lifts out easily for repairs or VCR hookup. Attractive wood-grain oilcloth-on-metal cabinet insures long-lasting good looks and protection from harmful radiation. Televoven controls are clearly marked and easy to work with (Instruction Tome Included). Although this versatile tool is particularly well suited to cramped trailers or studio apartments, many Televoven owners write Us that the sight of food cooking, or even water boiling, is a fascinating alternative to most television fare, no matter where it is watched. Full cable capability. Screen diameter 13″. Weight, 32 lbs.

TEEVEAT   Microwave Televoven, $542.25 ppd.

Headrest Antimacassar

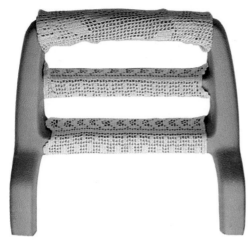

This handsome, hand-tied macrame headrest cover keeps hair treatments, dandruff, and natural secretions off most headrests; protects upholstery during whiplash, sitting up straight, or pulling over to the side of the road for a little snooze. Antimacassar unravels easily for convenient tieoff and custom fit. Hand Wash; never say Dry. Set of 2 weighs 8¼ oz.

NEATO   Headrest Antimacassar, $10.75 ppd.

Color, Doily.

Porto-Bib

Handy coverge for the travelling slob. Plastic Bib measures 12″ x 16″, gives maximum protection from dripping butter sauce, cole slaw, and other indiscreet foods. Folds up neatly into its own carrying case for easy transport to next refueling stop. Sturdy ties accept standard bow.
PORKO   Porto-Bib, $1.75 ppd.

Weight, 1¼ ounce.

Dress Bib

Luxurious, larger-than-full-size Bib covers shirt front when eating like a pig in elegant restaurants or decent homes. Hemmed edges resist frayage from wiping mouth or sucking gravy out of fabric. Bib ties in back with simple knot or may be tucked into loosened collar for casual flair at feeding time. Swirl pattern, cream-on-cream Damask is the same type found in many table cloths. Measures 15″ x 18″.
SLAHBO   Dress Bib, $6.25 ppd.

Weight, 2 oz.

Cuyahoga Grill

Innovative Grill does not need charcoal, lighter fluid, kindling, artificial logs, or wood. Its heavy three-section barrel is made of steel that has been blended with highly flammable industrial sludge, petroleum by-products, napalm, and sewage. Ignites on contact with any flame, or spontaneously, and provides a usually controllable, very hot burn, so meat cooks more quickly. Food cooked on this Grill has a distinctive charcoal-like flavor and is probably non-toxic. Barrel sections collapse for easy storage and blaze control. Double-sided nickel-plated Grill has extra-long handles for sure food grip through engulfing flames. Comes with Instruction Manual and five 14 oz. tubes of Unguentine. Extinguish carefully. Store away from any remotely flammable items. Weight, 43/5 lb. Collapsed size at room temperature: 12¼″ x 12¼″ x 6¼″. Expands when hot.

Weight, 43/5 lb.

SMOKY Cuyahoga Grill, $20.25 ppd.

Rabbit Fur Wallpaper

A handsome, practical wall covering, this natural French rabbit fur in various shadings of gray and brown is soft, warm, and moisture resistant. Quilted woolen lining provides additional insulation, cuts fuel costs. A small area of this Wallpaper in bedroom or bath will substantially reduce towel usage. Makes effective back scratcher as well. Comes with real glue.

HARE   Rabbit Fur Wallpaper, $178.25 ppd.

Instructions included for easy installation.

Weight per 5 yard roll, 15 lbs.

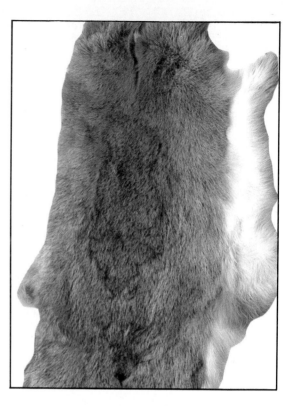

Home Paver

This is the finest hand-operated paving machine we have encountered. Hopper carries up to 75 lbs. of cement, macadam, asphalt, or gravel. Dispenses evenly for easy spreading. Heavy duty, braced handle reduces chance of hernia. Useful for making driveways and walkways, or for converting bothersome yard into trouble-free, low maintenance deck. (Paint green to reduce glare.). Wt. 72 lbs.

ROLLR   Home Paver, $198.40 ppd.

Poo-Bah™ Gradient Eyeglass Frames

Quality eyewear from Bash and Lob. Frames change shape according to light and social conditions. Gold-plated metal Aviator Frames hold lenses for shopping, harsh light or day, or aviation; Horn Rims at work, Sequined Harlequin Frames for evening or recreational wear. Send prescription or we will supply Our Own. Weight, Color, interesting questions.

PRESTO   Poo-Bah™ Gradient Eyeglass Frames, $43.25 ppd.

Truecheck Friendship Gauge

Accurately measures sincerity and depth of people's feelings. Sound waves, personal vibrations, and karmic nuances in atmosphere produce metric readout of subject's emotions and thoughts on a wide range of subjects of concern to many. Highly prized by doubting Thomases, Jewish mothers, and federal investigators, this is the best tool we know of to find out who's putting you on. Attaches in seconds. Instructions Included.

TRSTY   Truecheck Friendship Gauge, $139.50 ppd.

Weight, 3 lbs.
Color: Grey Area.

Our Singing Tea Kettles

Traditionally shaped Kettles cast in either iron or aluminum let you know when water is boiling by singing a tune. Many of Our customers use these on their wood stoves. They make excellent humidifiers and duet partners, and are usually cheaper to operate than radios. Each Kettle has a repertoire of 3–5 pieces and will improvise if properly warmed up. Tune selections depend on lid position, water level, and rapport with heat source. Two sizes in either black cast iron or rustproof cast aluminum.

Heavy Metal: Three and a half qt. cast iron Tea Kettle sings "Strange Brew," "Tea-ball Wizard," "Tea and Sympathy for the Devil," others.

D'VIDA   Heavy Metal Singing Tea Kettle, $38.75 ppd.

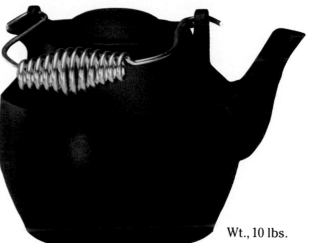

Wt., 10 lbs.

Wt., 15 lbs.

Robeson: Six qt. cast iron Tea Kettle sings "In Diesen Heil'gen Hallen," "Old Man River," others.

PRFNDO   Robeson Singing Tea Kettle, $47.25 ppd.

Blossom: Three and a half qt. cast aluminum Tea Kettle sings "Tea for Two," "One Cup for the Road," "April in South Paris," others.

DEAR   Blossom Singing Tea Kettle, $45.25 ppd.

Wt., 3 lbs.

Wt., 4½ lbs.

Placido: Six qt. cast aluminum Tea Kettle sings "Vesti La Giubba," "Lady of Spain," others.

M'APPARI   Placido Singing Tea Kettle, $69.75 ppd.

Persona-Fone

State-of-the-art electronic design allows this machine not only to answer, monitor, and record telephone calls, but to actually converse with callers. Voice-activated diodes start and stop a prerecorded cassette so imperceptibly that its sound quality is virtually indistinguishable from that of a live voice on the wire. Your cassette can make polite conversation, come straight to the point, evade the issue, avoid the issue, make excuses, stall, or scream vile, hysterical insults to suit personal preference, need, or style. Saves time and energy. Suggested Conversation Scripts Included. Unit plugs into any standard outlet.

BLABLA   Persona-Fone, $132.25 ppd.

Wt. about 3½ lbs.

Our Toilet Kit

Well-suited for use in the field or while travelling, this handsome Kit is made out of soft elk-tanned cowhide with a waterproof, vinyl-coated nylon lining. It contains a selection of supplies no one should ever be without no matter What. Contents: 1 Roll Toilet Paper (Two ply). 3 Wet Naps. Nail File. Vitamin Pills (430 assorted). 4 Band-Aids. Eye Patch. Tourniquet. 2 Toothbrushes (Morning and bedtime). 1 Small Tube Toothpaste. Shock-Corded Folding Cane. Plastic Laminate 4″ x 6″ Card Containing Metric Equivalency Chart and the Lord's Prayer. Esperanto Phrase Book, More Band-Aids. Fork. Knife. Spoon. Immersion Coil. 3 Bouillon Cubes (1 Beef, 1 chicken, 1 vegetable). 2 Tampons. 2 Condoms. 1 Ripstop Toilet Seat Cover with Stuff Sack. 1 Pair White Cotton Gloves. Eyedrops. Nose Drops. Ear Drops. Dew Drops. Pain Drops. Rain Drops. Dropsy Drops. Assorted Lozenges. 1 Chocolate Bar. Kit has handy, triple-stitched carrying loop, zip closure, hidden name tag with embossed registration number, and optional battery-powered burglar alarm. Ten inches long x 5″ wide x 4½″ high. Weight 8¼ lbs.

HYPO   Our Toilet Kit, $38.75 ppd.
EEK   Our Toilet Kit with Burglar Alarm, $48.25 ppd.

65

Home Intercom

Energy saving indoor communication system saves breath used in shouting up and down stairs, from room to room or just outside home, cottage, or camp. Good-looking, well-polished 6 oz. juice-type tin cans are lidless at one end, connected to each other with 20 ft. of professional quality, white cotton string at the other. Talking into can transmits sound effortlessly along full length of string. Cans make excellent receivers as well. Non-electric, non-mechanical construction with no moving parts uses no energy, so Intercom is very inexpensive to operate. Wall– ceiling mounting hooks keep string off floor, preventing tangleage. Cans wipe clean with damp cloth. String is removable for washing and ease in unravelling. Additional cans and string Available. Set of 2 cans and 20′ of string weigh less than a lb. Not recommended for use around corners.

LOTECH Home Intercom, $3.75 ppd.

Cruise Missile

Highly maneuverable, non-exploding Missile can fly at moderate speeds along beaches, in bars, or around parties. Asks questions, makes casual conversation, or silently gets lay of land for subsequent debriefing at home base. Compact Missile, roll-up launch pad and remote controls are small enough to fit in car trunk. Handy way to explore new situations without threat of disappointment or embarrassment. Missile is 4′2″ and weighs about 118.531 lbs. Partial assembly Required. Color: Hiya Silver.

U-2? Cruise Missile, $591.25 ppd.

Executive Communications Module

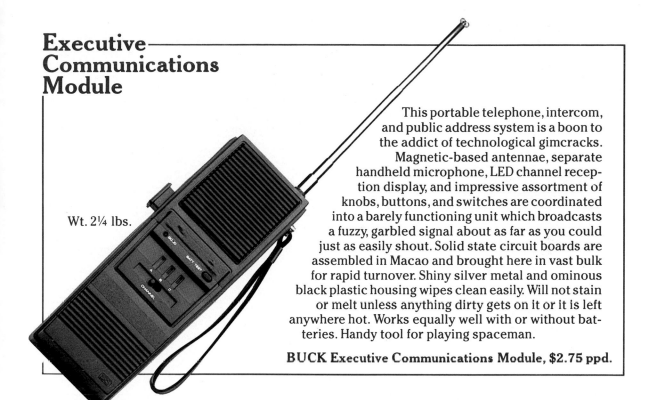

Wt. 2¼ lbs.

This portable telephone, intercom, and public address system is a boon to the addict of technological gimcracks. Magnetic-based antennae, separate handheld microphone, LED channel reception display, and impressive assortment of knobs, buttons, and switches are coordinated into a barely functioning unit which broadcasts a fuzzy, garbled signal about as far as you could just as easily shout. Solid state circuit boards are assembled in Macao and brought here in vast bulk for rapid turnover. Shiny silver metal and ominous black plastic housing wipes clean easily. Will not stain or melt unless anything dirty gets on it or it is left anywhere hot. Works equally well with or without batteries. Handy tool for playing spaceman.

BUCK Executive Communications Module, $2.75 ppd.

Personal Stereo System

State-of-the-art Stereo System provides rich sound without the discomfort and inconvenience of headphones or console. Speakers are built into two good-looking rings which can be worn on left and right hands for full stereo separation. Deck is built into handsome, well-made belt buckle that will fit any normal, 1⅜″ belt (Not included). Experiment with different arm positions for optimum sound quality. Cup hands over ears when private listenage is desired. System decreases vulnerability to muggers, allows more attentive driving, and greatly expands opportunities for nodding or dancing to music.

B'LONY Personal Stereo System, $89.25 ppd.

Weight, ⅛ lb.

Dorian Spray Age Retardant

Handy aerosol spray halts aging process up to 12 hours. No wheezing, drooping, or other surprises when bounding up stairs or losing temper on tennis court. Balding, crow's feet, and general wrinklage are stopped. Muscles and mental capacity remain firm, strong, and pliant. Our Guarantee does not apply in case of overdose, which may result in prolonged adolescence followed by premature senility. Very useful item for parties, job interview, or life in the fast lane. Eleven ounce spray can is able to turn back hands of time up to 16 yrs. Store in cool, dark place for extended life on and off shelf.

OSKY Dorian Spray Age Retardant, $19.00 ppd.

Before   After

Writer's Crampon

Blocked students, journalists, fictionalists, and amanuenses will appreciate this pliable foam grip which allows comfortable perchage on pen or pencil with shaking, clenched, or twitching fingers. Adjustable implement groove holds all standard size writing tools as well as most erasers. Not recommended for use with quill pens or word processors. Lightweight non-allergenic foam can withstand many hours of continuous kneading, chewing, or inactivity. Many of Our Staff use these when paying bills, filling out tax forms, or writing post cards home from cottage, camp, or motel. Hand Wash. Line Dry.

Weight, 3 oz.

Color: Doughty White.

SCRBL Writer's Crampon, $5.00 ppd.

Navel Reamer

Gently but thoroughly cleans and buffs navel interior. Hand operated, rotary action, all-cotton buff pad is mounted on gimbal-type suspension system for painless adjustment to innies, outies, or unusually shaped navels. Replacement buff pad Available. Frequent use of this grooming aid improves self-contemplation skills as well as insuring hygienic receptacle for salt when eating celery in bed.

LNT   Navel Reamer, $18.75 ppd.

Wt., 3 oz.

Full Strength Eyeglass Snug

Lightweight, adjustable Snug insures secure eyeglass placement during active sports, sporting activities, yard work, or general gapage. Straps attach firmly to frames with clear propylene loops to maintain constant tension. Loosen immediately in case of migraine or dizziness. Adhesive nose bridge guards (Included) attach inconspicuously to most frame styles for added comfort. Straps blend nicely with face and head. Highly Recommended for athletes, nerds, and enthusiastic head shakers or nodders. Wt. 3 oz.

DWEEB   Full Strength Eyeglass Snug, $11.50 ppd.

69

Trainer Bongos

Beat, hippy, and former beat or hippy parents will enjoy watching their off-spring's first experiences with rhythm, coordination and *la vie bohème* with these excellent quality miniature Bongo drums. Natural skin heads stay tight, will maintain powerful tone long enough to give many parents severe headaches. Eventual breakage Guaranteed. Set comes with little Hippy-Dippy Beard and Extra-small beret.

Color: Babywood and Boogiewood Veneer.

GOOBOP   Trainer Bongo Drums, $11.75 ppd.

Weight, 1¾ lbs.

Our Decals

These Transfer Decals are made from pure chemical dyes and are treated for weather resistance and color intensity. They go on painlessly and fade in 3 – 5 days, if kept completely dry. Illustrated Instructions Included. We offer two types of decals: Our Decorative Tattoo-type Decals are based on traditional Coney Island designs. Authentic, pin-pricked appearance. Skillfully applied, one or more of these rakish Tattoos will make the weediest runt look like the Marlboro Man. Not recommended for formal wear or the clergy.
Set of 4: Mother I Love You. Base Camp: Hell. Born to Bivouac. Camouflage.
Our Label Decals save time and trouble for the absent-minded, conceptually oriented, or simply stupid person by providing neat, concise labels for difficult-to-remember body parts.
Set of 6: Head. Hand. Arm. Leg. Chest. Duodenum.

BIFF   Our Decorative Tattoo-Type Decals, $4.75 ppd.
QUOI   Our Label Decals, $4.75 ppd.

Personal Spotlight

This handy portable Spotlight provides self-illumination while telling jokes, monopolizing conversation, or distracting others. Pocket-type size, sturdy clip-on clip, and flexible, vinyl-covered gooseneck leaves hands free for expressive flailing, flamboyant breast-beating, or sensitive cigarette handleage. Adjustable beam narrows to tiny pin spot suitable for confessions, revelations, or propositions. 20W tungsten-halogen bulb will burn brightly through many hours of self-aggrandizement.

DESMOND   Personal Spotlight, $10.00 ppd.

Weight 2 oz.
Color: Bronzish Electroplate.

Eyeglass Wipers

Highly recommended for walking in the rain, taking steam baths, and watching pornographic films, these miniature Wipers clip on to virtually any type of eyeglasses to provide clear vision under wet, misty, or steamy conditions. One nth horsepower, defroster fan, cleaning fluid ampule and sprayer fit compactly alongside bridge of nose, while H-type battery, on/off switch, and function controls slip conveniently in or behind ears. Tiny ice scraper and brush included for cold weather lens maintenance.

4/I'S   Eyeglass Wipers, $14.25 ppd.

Wt., ¼ lb.

Our Oak Accessories

Handsome and functional Accessories made in Maine of durable oak, oak veneer, and reconstituted oak shavings. Hand-sanded and finished to a long-lasting, hand-sanded finish. To clean, wipe with a damp cloth or resand and refinish. In either case, let dry before using.

Oak Toilet Tissue, Paper Towel, and Tissue Canisters: Constructed of various types of oak with plastic liners and tight fitting lids, these sturdy Canisters keep utility papers clean, dry, and out of sight. Set of 3 Canisters weighs 11 lbs.

SANTÉ   Oak Toilet Tissue, Paper Towel, and Tissue Canisters, $22.50 ppd.

Oak Notion Set: Traditionally designed for a variety of household jobs, set includes 3 Toothpicks, 2 Chopsticks, 4 Tongue Depressors (Unflavored), 6 Swab Shafts (Cotton not included), and 8 unpainted domino blanks. Set will last for generations if properly cared for (Instructions Included). Weight, ½ lb.

VARIÉ
Oak Notion Set,
$7.75 ppd.

Freckle Template

Permits controlled development of facial freckles. Form-fitting Bakelite mask covers face completely, allowing sun and wind only through precut dots. Freckle hue is easily regulated by amount of sun or lamp time spent with Template in position. Remove while tanning to adjust base tone. One piece, contoured Template may be trimmed to accommodate individual faces. File edges smooth with orange stick or rasp. Lack of eyeholes makes Template unsuitable for costume wear.

Three Freckle Styles: Cute. Traditional Dappled. Deeply Speckled.

HOWDY Freckle Template, $3.75 ppd.

Weight, 6⅜ oz.

Cheese Flavored Tongue Depressors

A favorite of pediatricians and eye, ear, nose, and throat men, these well-made, solid maple Depressors are coated with a fine spray of tasty, cold-pack process cheese food for a handy snack while being examined. Traditionally designed Depressors are ½″ wide at both ends for easy grip and unobstructed view of soft palate, uvula, wind pipe, and mucous membranes. Finely chopped, they make an interesting addition to salads or cold buffets. Chew carefully before swallowing. Refrigerate after opening. Box of 100 Tongue Depressors weighs about 1 lb.

Four flavors: Cheddar. Cheddar with Port. Finnish Swiss. Gorgonzola. Assorted. (Gorgonzola flavored Depressors not recommended for close examinations.)

SAYAH Cheddar Flavored Tongue Depressors, $4.45 ppd.
SAYAAH Cheddar with Port Flavored Tongue Depressors, $4.45 ppd.
SAYAAÄH Finnish Swiss Flavored Tongue Depressors, $4.45 ppd.
SAYUGH Gorgonzola Flavored Tongue Depressors, $4.45 ppd.
PHEU Assorted Cheese Flavored Tongue Depressors, $4.45 ppd.

Lifetime Letter Opener

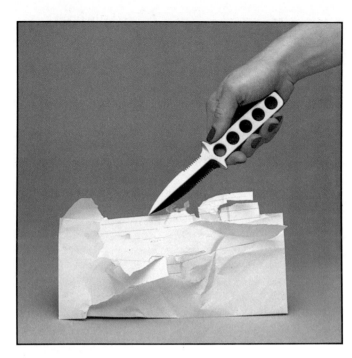

Unusual Opener is precision ground from a solid block of vanadium steel, the hardest substance on this page. Slices easily through thick Jetpacks, knotted string, or heavily taped packages, yet is thin and responsive enough to handle onion skin envelopes, air letters, or gift wrap. Dual-edged blade is razor sharp, with serrated teeth at base for cutting heavy cord or duct tape. Safety sheath may be clipped to belt or boot for immediate access when quick mail openage is necessary or desired. Weight 5 oz. with sheath. Opener is made in Finland, where opening mail is an art, and comes with a Lifetime Guarantee (Not covered by Our Guarantee).

POSTIA   Lifetime Letter Opener, $39.75 ppd.

———— Our Matches ————

These convenient paper items are the easiest way we know of to produce a manageable amount of fire without special equipment. To use, remove individual sulphur-tipped paper stick from book one at a time. Run tip across friction board until flame appears. Use flame to light cigarettes, candles, ovens, etc. Our Matches come in handy books of twenty to thirty; no two are exactly alike. Many of Our Staff keep Matches on their persons as well as at home, cottage, or camp. They are useful for odd jobs or just to light one at a time, drop into an ash tray, and stare at until they burn out. Please close cover before striking. Set of 5 weighs 2 oz.

Two book patterns: Our Logo. Camouflage.

FLAMR   Our Matches, $.50 ppd.

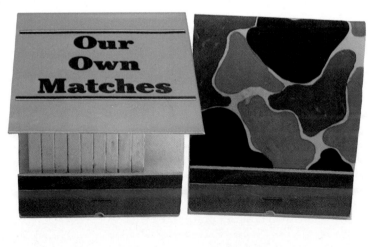

Sheepskin Swabs

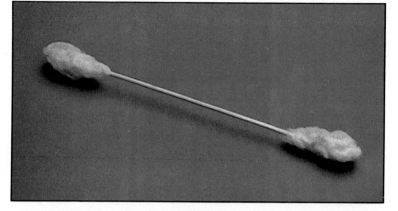

We have received many requests over the years for an extra-durable Swab that would stand up to many of the hard jobs for which traditional cotton models are too fragile, including cleaning very dirty ears, buffing hard-to-reach boot tongues, and applying old, well-caked unguents of all types.

After weeks of research, We are introducing this heavy duty Swab made from imported Merino Sheepskin. Absorbent, high loft fleece holds large quantities of powder, paste, or what-have-youage with ease. Fleece tips are hand-fitted to solid oak shaft which is heavily varnished to a smooth, protective finish. Alcohol, hot liquids, and kerosene-based thinners will not stain. Properly cared for, a few of these Swabs will provide years of service and considerable savings in regular swab costs. Tips detach for easy cleaning. Hand Wash and Air Dry. Shafts wipe clean with a dry cloth. Replacement tips available. Made to fit Our Swab Covers. Wt. 1 nth oz. Color: Naturelle.

MR. CL   Sheepskin Swab, $3.25 ppd.

Commuter's Spittoon

Makes inconspicuous a habit considered repulsive by many. Flip-top lid with no-spill funnel rim conceals accumulated gobbets completely, also unscrews easily for emptyage and sterilization. Interesting conversation piece as well as truly considerate item for car-poolers. Washable brown and beige plastic resembles many commuter's-type coffee mugs. Two models: Standard Handled and Professional Type with No Handle. Professional Type Spittoon fits easily into brief case or attaché but requires better aim than Standard Handled Model.

P'   Standard Handled Commuter's Spittoon, $4.25 ppd.
TOOEY   Professional Type Commuter's Spittoon, $4.25 ppd.

Each holds 8 oz. and weighs 4 oz.

Bicycle Seat Comforter

Soft, comfortable Merino Sheepskin Bicycle Seat Comforter wraps fully around hard, narrow bicycle seats and makes them possible to use. Merino wool is thicker than other wools, a fact that will be much appreciated by hemorrhoid sufferers, well-endowed men, or pretty much anyone who rides a bicycle. Wt., 8 oz.

BMPTY   Bicycle Seat Comforter, $32.25 ppd.

Color: Pale Lamb.

Deluxe Toilet Seat Cover

Similar in design to Our Ripstop Toilet Seat Cover, this Deluxe Model is intended for home use. It is made of specially selected Merino Sheepskin with an extra-soft finish for maximum cushioning and warmth during elimination, procrastination, or just passing the time. High loft fleece allows free air movement around buttocks, reducing moisture buildup and providing a more comfortable, cuddly seat. Generously sized Cover is mildew resistant, non-allergenic, and has an elasticized edge for snug fit. Hand wash and Air Dry.

CUSH   Deluxe Toilet Seat Cover, $50.25 ppd.

Weight, 1½ lb.
Color: Royal Flushed.

EWE Sheepskin Bud Vase,
$36.50 ppd.

Sheepskin Bud Vase and Fruit Bowl ——————————

These best grade, imported Merino sheepskin re-
ceptacles hold fruit, floral arrangements, and other
decorative items. Bark-tanned skins contain no
corrosive chemicals and are lightly caulked to
prevent leakage. Bud Vase comes
with mounting hardware for installation as wall sconce. Fruit
Bowl may be displayed fleecy
side out as shown.
    Color: Sheepish.

BET   Sheepskin Fruit Bowl,
$47.75 ppd.

Heavy Duty Finials

Aluminun alloy Finials with brass-like or natural aluminum finish provide balanced and secure fastenage for lampshades of all sorts. Stainless steel thread linings have been spin bored rather than force fit for better hold on mounting hardware. Properly cared for, these Finials should last for years, making sloppy, unsafe lampshade installation a thing of the past. Traditional Bemused Eagle design looks well atop all lamps. Set of 2 Finials weighs 6 oz. Choice of 2 colors: Brass-like. Natural Aluminum. Please give second choice with order.

WIDGT   Heavy Duty Finials, $3.75 ppd.

Long Haul Gear Shift Knobs

Designed for heavy use by truckers, bootleggers, and auto enthusiasts, these Knobs fit all standard shift levers and are hollow inside to provide a handy, inconspicuous cache for change, good luck charms, and health aids. High gloss enamel on metal with "no-seam" hinging is attractive and undetectable in case of unexpected search and seizure.

Five colors: Snow White. Black Beauty. Red Devil. Vitamin C Orange. Toll Silver.

RT66   Long Haul Gear Shift Knobs, $11.25 ppd.

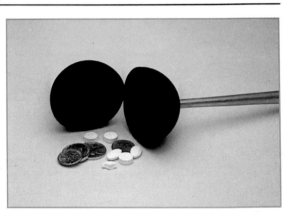

Wt., 5 oz.

Battery and Film Packs
(For Refrigerator Doors)

Batteries and film last longer when they are kept at low temperatures, but frequently cause unconscionable clutter in many refrigerators, freezers, and wine cellars. We make these handy containers for the homemaker who would like to keep batteries and film cold without creating a mess. Each Pack holds six batteries or packages of film and will fit easily in any refrigerator door compartment. Avoids confusion with battery- or film-shaped foods or beverages.

Three Battery Pack sizes: AA. C. D.

SPIC   Battery Pack, $3.50 ppd.
SPAN   Film Pack, $3.50 ppd.

Three Film Pack Sizes: 35mm. 110 Cartridge. Polaroid.

—"White Lie" Paper— Shredders

The small firm of Gorsuch and Liddy of Sleazeville, Colorado, has been making these crank-operated Paper Shredders since 1923. Handsome, maple-stained white pine tub fits easily under desk or blends with virtually any décor. Shredding apparatus and crank drive are removable for easy cleaning and concealment. Surgical steel shredders will slice documents into unreadable 5/32" strips. Easy crank action provides light upper body exercise for operator. Ideal Shredder for the small businessman.

Government officials and corporate executives may prefer the Motor Drive Paper Shredder. Quiet but efficient motor generates enough power to handle official reports, appointment calendars, and other bulky incriminatage. Five and a half foot electric cord detaches for emergency use as garrote or noose in case of unexpected disclosure.

RITA "Secretary" Crank-Operated Paper Shredder, $89.50 ppd.

ANNE "Executive" Crank-Operated Paper Shredder, $108.25 ppd.

DADOO "Secretary" Motor Drive Paper Shredder, $212.78 ppd.

RONRON "Executive" Motor Drive Paper Shredder, $272.75 ppd.

Two size buckets: "Executive" (6 Qt.). "Secretary" (4 Qt.).
Two Styles: Hand Crank-Operated. Motor drive.

Our Samplers

These hand-embroidered Samplers are individually made by New England fishermen's widows. Each displays a saying or reminder that gives these handsome decorative items a practical side as well. Measures 18″ x 21″. Ample margins for framing.

Three Samplers: "PILL." "TURN ON MACHINE." "CALM DOWN!!!" Please give second choice with order.

IFORGT   Our Sampler, $23.25 ppd.

Moosehide Toothbrush Case

Supple yet protective moosehide leather is hand-sewn to make this strong, light-weight, and well-ventilated Case for tooth-brush carryage on the trail. Leather laces adjust for snug fit. Belt loops and hand-cut ventiports across top of Case allow fresh air to waft over brush when not in use. Recommended unanimously by the Presque Isle Dental Association for use with both hard and soft bristle brushes.

PLAQ   Moosehide Toothbrush Case, $5.25 ppd.

First Lady Floor Wax

This is the same Wax First Ladies have used for years when scrubbing floors at White House, cottage, or Camp David. Made up in small batches according to a Classified formula, it is concentrated for easy polishing without unseemly wax or arm buildup. Comes in good looking ½ gallon stoneware crock with a laminated, autographed letter from the First Lady urging kind thoughts for the world's oppressed. Mopping Instructions Included.

**CROCK
First Lady Floor Wax, $18.50 ppd.**

Wt., ⅛ oz.

Invisible Woman of Borneo

Imported, flesh-and-blood human being makes stealthy spy or handy household helper. Each belongs to a sect which, through centuries of quaint ceremony and herb intake, has mastered ability to disappear. Light-footed tread enables Woman to snoop anywhere that is not electronically secured. Makes excellent magician's assistant. Cooks, cleans, and does other light work. Does not do windows. Wages and contract negotiable (Not covered by Our Guarantee). Woman comes dressed in versatile knit shirtdress with three-button placketed neck and grosgrain D-ring belt for good visibility when unwrapping. Wt., 98–115 lbs.

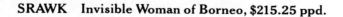

Color: None.

SRAWK   Invisible Woman of Borneo, $215.25 ppd.

—Happy Illusion Survival Kit

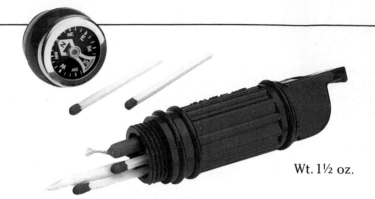

Made with the same quality workmanship found in many party favors and cereal box prizes, this combination tool includes three absorbing distractions for the helpless or doomed camper. Toy compass has a plainly marked, luminous dial, and may indicate true north from time to time. Almost watertight match compartment is large enough to hold several matches, one birthday candle, a joint (Not included), and small prayer (Included). Whistle produces light, pleasant tootle for whiling away final hours or signalling too softly for help. Instructions for playing "Taps" Included. Bright red plastic is pretty as well as visible to fading eyesight. Although none of Kit's functions are covered by Our Guarantee, we recommend this item for the diversion it offers to children playing make-believe as well as disintegrating outdoorsmen facing the end.

Wt. 1½ oz.

R.I.P. Happy Illusion Survival Kit, $6.25

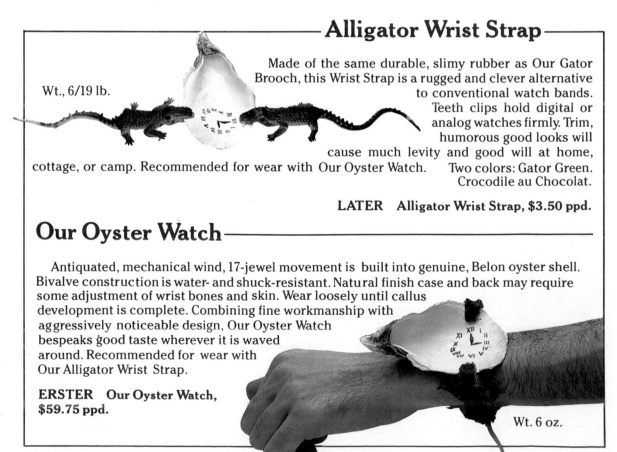

Alligator Wrist Strap—

Wt., 6/19 lb.

Made of the same durable, slimy rubber as Our Gator Brooch, this Wrist Strap is a rugged and clever alternative to conventional watch bands. Teeth clips hold digital or analog watches firmly. Trim, humorous good looks will cause much levity and good will at home, cottage, or camp. Recommended for wear with Our Oyster Watch. Two colors: Gator Green. Crocodile au Chocolat.

LATER   Alligator Wrist Strap, $3.50 ppd.

Our Oyster Watch———

Antiquated, mechanical wind, 17-jewel movement is built into genuine, Belon oyster shell. Bivalve construction is water- and shuck-resistant. Natural finish case and back may require some adjustment of wrist bones and skin. Wear loosely until callus development is complete. Combining fine workmanship with aggressively noticeable design, Our Oyster Watch bespeaks good taste wherever it is waved around. Recommended for wear with Our Alligator Wrist Strap.

ERSTER   Our Oyster Watch, $59.75 ppd.

Wt. 6 oz.

82